Machine Politics, Sound Bites, and Nostalgia: On Studying Political Parties

Machine Politics, Sound Bites, and Nostalgia: On Studying Political Parties

Edited by
Michael Margolis
and
John C. Green

Prepared by
The Ray C. Bliss Institute of Applied Politics
The University of Akron

UNIVERSITY
PRESS OF
AMERICA

Lanham • New York • London

THE RAY C. BLISS
INSTITUTE OF
APPLIED POLITICS
The University of Akron
Akron, Ohio

University Press of America®, Inc.
4720 Boston Way
Lanham, Maryland 20706

3 Henrietta Street
London WC2E 8LU England

Co-published by arrangement with
The Ray C. Bliss Institute of Applied Politics

Library of Congress Cataloging-in-Publication Data

Machine politics, sound bites, and nostalgia : on studying
political parties / edited by Michael Margolis and
John C. Green ; prepared by the Ray C. Bliss Institute
of Applied Politics, the University of Akron.
p.   cm.
1. Political parties—United States—Congresses.   2. Politics,
Practical—United States—Congresses.   I. Margolis, Michael.
II. Green, John C.   III. Ray C. Bliss Institute of Applied Politics.
JK2265.M25   1992   324.273—dc20   92–32648 CIP

ISBN 0–8191–8855–7 (cloth : alk. paper)
ISBN 0–8191–8856–5 (pbk. : alk. paper)

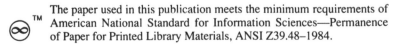

The paper used in this publication meets the minimum requirements of
American National Standard for Information Sciences—Permanence
of Paper for Printed Library Materials, ANSI Z39.48–1984.

Contents

Tables

Preface

The Political Organization and Parties Section of the American Political Science Association sponsored the first of perhaps many research workshops on Wednesday, August 28, 1991. Entitled "Machine Politics, Soundbites, and Nostalgia: Substantive Issues and Methodological Problems in the Study of Party Organization," the workshop included a panel of scholars presenting brief papers on research questions and a panel of practitioners responding from their personal experience. The results of these panels are included in this publication, the goal of which is to make the results of the workshop available to students of political parties.

This first workshop was the product of several years of discussion and many months of preparation. Special recognition must be given to the leadership of POP, particularly Margaret Conway, Chair of the section, Ruth Jones, the Program Chair. Michael Margolis served with distinction as the Workshop Coordinator, while Paul Herrnson provided invaluable assistance in organizing the panels, and Michael Brintnall of the APSR contributed logistical support. We are grateful to the participating scholars and practitioners who graciously consented to have their remarks reprinted here. Special thanks goes to Kimberly Haverkamp of the Bliss Institute for her careful work on the manuscript.

The Ray C. Bliss Institute of Applied Politics is a bipartisan research institute at The University of Akron, dedicated to understanding the "nuts and bolts" of practical politics with a particular emphasis on political parties. Thus we are pleased to help make the results of the POP workshop available to the broader community of scholars. We hope to provide a similar service for future POP workshops.

John C. Green, Director
Bliss Institute

About The Contributors

Lewis Bowman, retired from the University of South Florida, is Professor of Political Science at the University of North Texas. He has done extensive research on local party politics.

Leon Epstein, Professor Emeritus at the University of Wisconsin-Madison, is the author of *Political Parties in Western Democracies* (1967) and *Political Parties in the American Mold* (1986). He is a past-president of the American Political Science Association (1978-79).

Charles D. Hadley, Research Professor of Political Science at the University of New Orleans, is the co-author of *Transformations of the American Party System* (1978).

Paul Herrnson, Associate Professor of Political Science at the University of Maryland, is the author of *Party Campaigning in the 1980s* (1988).

Kay Lawson, Professor of Political Science at San Francisco State University, is the author of *The Comparative Study of Political Parties* (1976) and co-editor of *When Parties Fail* (1988).

Michael Margolis, Professor of Political Science at the University of Cincinnati, is the author of *Viable Democracy* (1979) and co-editor of *Manipulating Public Opinion* (1988).

PART ONE

Scholarly Perspectives

Overview of Research on
Party Organizations

Leon D. Epstein

Asked to discuss briefly the state of research on party organizations, principally understood as state and local organizations, I shall first comment generally and then cite only a few studies to illustrate the extensive scholarly literature on the subject.

My perspective these days is principally that of a synthesizing user of the organizational research conducted by others. It is about 35 years since I studied party organizations in Wisconsin counties, employing interviews, mail questionnaires, and participant-observations (Epstein 1958: Chapter 5). That experience, together with a nearly simultaneous study of candidate-selection practices of British constituency associations, convinced me of both the value and the arduousness of such research. At the time of my Wisconsin work, political scientists in other states were also studying the new ideological activist organizations that seemed to be replacing patronage parties. Some of these studies, completed in the early 1960s, were widely recognized as important scholarship; striking examples are the books written by Samuel Eldersveld (1964) and James Q. Wilson (1962). Their work maintained a traditional professional concern with party organizations as key elements in understanding the democratic political process. That concern goes back to Ostrogorski (1902) and Michels (1915), and it includes landmark studies of old party machines like Chicago's (Gosnell 1937). Surely, the profession's concern with the subject persists, as all of us know and as I shall emphasize in discussing work of the last decade. Nevertheless, studies of party organizations appear less salient since the mid-1960s or thereabouts. I mean not only less salient in political science generally, where of course the development of many new fields reduces the relative importance of parties, but also less salient even within the parties field itself. I believe that more time and energy are devoted to party systems, party competition, party voters, party identifiers, and legislative parties than to extra-governmental party organizations.

Perhaps research on party organizations, especially at state and local levels, has not been the readiest path to fame and fortune for political scientists during the last quarter century. That supposition can be supported by at least one crude measure: among 238 articles and research notes appearing in twenty issues of the *American Political Science Review* during a recent five-year period (March 1986 through December 1990), only one--a research note--was devoted to extra-governmental party organization at any level in the United States or elsewhere. This statistic may reflect more than the fact that party organization is but one of the multitude of subjects now attracting political scientists. Research on organizations ordinarily requires field work, either by a principal investigator or through specially developed survey instruments, while scholars are understandably tempted by inquiries that can be pursued by using already available data from established surveys, documents, and secondary sources, or by philosophical and methodological work for which no empirically-derived data are needed. Thus, only a modest percentage of *APSR* articles *on any subject*, I once observed in the mid-1980s, contain newly gathered data from elite interviews, participant-observation, or specially developed surveys or questionnaires (as distinct from national surveys used in many voting-behavior articles).

The very state and local character of party organizations may also help account for the subject's lack of prominence. Political scientists, like many Americans, are likely to be more interested in national than in state and local affairs. To some extent, that interest is reflected in useful and important studies of national party organizations. Their recent expansion surely justifies attention, and the availability of campaign finance data from the Federal Election Commission facilitates relevant research. Hence, it is harder than ever to persuade a Ph.D. candidate in the parties field to forgo the greater visibility of a national study in favor of studying state and local organizations. Yet good reasons remain for looking to sub-national units for most party organizational activity. We are far from certain that state and local parties have declined as conventional wisdom suggests, and we still know too little about the non-patronage organizations that have developed, ever since the 1950s, to serve different purposes from those of the old machines. Several examples of new developments will be found in the excellent studies in Pomper (1980).

Characteristic of most recent scholarship is the realization that party organizations have had to accommodate to a candidate-centered political culture and particularly to a nominating process that they cannot control but may seek only to influence. The significance of this point is readily understood in comparative context. Everywhere outside the United States, party organizations, at one level or another but usually local or regional, control the bestowing of their party labels; that is to say, dues paying party members or their chosen executive committees select (nominate) candidates.

Only in the United States do laws turn over candidate selection by parties to voters, whose commitment to party is no more than a legal registration or declaration in order to participate in primaries. Direct-primary laws, apart from their other effects, are thus widely believed to have reduced the power of party organizations and therefore also to have reduced a principal motivation for individuals to become regular and active party members.

In this context are many studies of how party organizations cope with nominating problems in the late twentieth-century American environment. Malcolm Jewell (1984) provides a leading example in his careful exploration of five of the several states whose parties used endorsing conventions to influence gubernatorial primaries in 1982. Viewing the pre-primary endorsing convention as an increasingly popular device for party activists, Jewell finds it to have organizational advantages, measured in part by the satisfaction that convention delegates expressed about their roles when answering questionnaires. Success in winning primaries for endorsed choices was, however, by no means uniform. Nor, it should be added, was organizational control of nominations anywhere near uniform during previous decades of direct-primary experience. Thus, Mayhew (1986) shows that traditional party organizations, while surviving in strength until the 1960s, had not been pervasively present and effective (even earlier in the century).

Most of the organizational research from the 1980s that I have encountered does not deal directly with Jewell's subject. More typical, I believe, is the use of surveys to learn about the backgrounds, motivations, and activities of party members. Crotty (1986) has edited an excellent set of studies of party committee members in five cities (Chicago, Detroit, Los Angeles, Houston, and Nashville). Among the findings are: continuing and even increasing activity during recent years in the first three cities; better Republican than Democratic organization in Houston and sometimes elsewhere; greater non-patronage incentives except in Chicago, with motivations most often provided by policy commitments; an adaptability of party organizations to changing ethnic populations; and a general loyalty of activists to their party despite their own occasional ticket-splitting. Incidentally, Crotty's book includes a chapter by Eldersveld that exemplifies his continuing research leadership in the party organizational field.

Inferentially at least, the relatively substantial organizational activity reported by the several studies in Crotty suggest that incentives for party participation remain despite the impact of the direct primary and of candidate-centered politics. Indeed, in Los Angeles the weakness of organizational power in matters like nominations is specifically cited to indicate that activists are attracted despite the weakness. A similar point is more explicit in Mildred Schwartz's study of the Illinois Republican Party (1990). She rejects the view of Mayhew (1986) and the Advisory Commission on Intergovernmental Relations (1986) that the older control of nominations is a key criterion in measuring organizational success. Thus, Schwartz finds that the Illinois Republican organization is effective even though its role in nominating contests falls short of regular control of outcomes. Her research is notable for its many and repeated interviews with various sets of party actors at various levels; these actors include government officeholders as well as party committee members. They supply both tabular data and apt quotations.

With its focus on a state party organization, Schwartz's work, as one reviewer (Flinn 1991) points out, may represent a shift from the conventional belief in the centrality of the county organization in the American party system. Schwartz is not alone in studying state organizations during the last decade. Jewell has been noted already. And there is also the NSF-funded, nation-wide Party Transformation Study by Cotter, Gibson, Bibby, and Huckshorn (1984), best known for its measures of the organizational strength and the professional bureaucratization of the several state parties. It does, however, devote a substantial chapter to local party organizations, in which the authors report considerable county-level activity bolstering the book's principal thesis that party organizations have not recently declined but have in some respects become more significant since the 1960s. Thus, even if state parties have become a primary focus for organizational research, local parties remain within the scope of inquiry. An apt illustration is provided by the one piece on party organization that I found in the twenty issues of the *APSR* noted earlier; it was a research note on "The Electoral Relevance of Local Party Organizations" by Frendreis, Gibson, and Vertz (1990) and it drew on data from the Party Transformation Study.

The Party Transformation Study, in its several published products, illustrates another characteristic of recent research on party organizations: an emphasis on gathering information that can be quantified and tabulated. For Cotter, Gibson, Bibby, and Huckshorn, numerous questionnaires produced this kind of information, although their research also involved interviews with certain party officials. Mail questionnaires are reasonably economic means for learning about party activists, and they have been used along with personal interviews in the several well-known studies of national convention delegates. Large-scale work of this kind is by Miller and Jennings (1986), and in Miller (1988). They have returns from Republican and Democratic delegates to the conventions of 1972 through 1984, and accordingly a wealth of data on their degree of party commitment, class background, motivational bases, and ideological positions. On the last of these, in particular, Miller and Jennings are able to show significant differences not only between Republican and Democratic delegates but also between each party's delegates and its electoral supporters (whose opinions are revealed in established surveys of the national electorate). Their work is perhaps the most elaborate of the several national convention delegate studies that began thirty years ago. Although such studies do not directly explore what party organizations do, they certainly tell us a good deal about the nature of party organizations--or at least about the nature of *presidential* party organizations. County chairs, Baer and Bositis (1988) have found, are ideologically distinguishable, especially on the Democratic side, from national convention delegates.

Referring to Baer and Bositis reminds me to observe that their book includes, along with research data, a useful discussion of how crucial organizational studies are to the maintenance of a distinguishable parties field. Without such studies, we might have only party-related research in other fields--legislative behavior, presidential or gubernatorial leadership, and voting behavior. Tendencies in that direction may help explain recent departmental difficulties in recruiting parties specialists among new Ph.Ds. Already, scholars primarily identified with other fields do a large share of the research of concern to students of parties. For example, legislative behavior specialists have much to tell us about the recently strengthened legislative parties, particularly their campaign committees. The importance of these office-holder parties, as well as those of governors and presidents, is apparent, and so is their often vexed relationship to ideologically oriented extra-governmental parties. Nothing, of course, precludes parties specialists from studying office-holder parties along with extra-governmental parties, and some of us have tried to do so.

Yet, it seems clear that it is the extra-governmental organizations that lie at the heart of our field. It is also clear that a renewed concern with these organizations must be based on evidence of their actual activity. Are they substantial and active enough so as to be effective in a candidate centered political culture? Here, recent research findings are reassuring. All of the scholarship that I have observed, in this paper and elsewhere, points to a continuing and even increasing organizational presence. Only the most skeptical would dismiss the findings as products of an over-identification of scholars with the subject matter of their research. It is true that party scholars welcome the signs of strength that they discover, and that a few even share and seek to promote the organizational activism that they study. Nevertheless, the scholarly evidence is persuasive at least with respect to the presence of substantial numbers of activists committed to party organizations. Less but still something is known about influence in nominations and election campaigns. To learn as much about the latter as about the characteristics and beliefs of organizational participants will require field work in addition to the sample surveys and mail questionnaires that now provide impressive quantifiable data.

References

Advisory Commission on Intergovernmental Relations. 1986. *The Transformation in American Politics*. Washington: ACIR.

Baer, Denise L., and Bositis, David A. 1988. *Elite Cadres and Party Coalitions*. New York: Greenwood Press.

Cotter, Corelius P., Gibson, James L., Bibby, John F., and Huckshorn, Robert J. 1984. *Party Organizations in American Politics*. New York: Praeger.

Crotty, William, ed. 1986. *Political Parties in Local Areas*. Knoxville: University of Tennessee Press.

Eldersveld, Samuel J. 1964. *Political Parties*. Chicago: Rand McNally.

Epstein, Leon D. 1958. *Politics in Wisconsin*. Madison: University of Wisconsin Press, 1958.

Flinn, Thomas A. 1991. Review of Mildred Schwartz, *The Party Network, American Political Science Review* 85:654-55.

Frendreis, John P., Gibson, James L., and Vertz, Laura L. 1990. "The Electoral Relevance of Local Party Organizations." *American Political Science Review*. 84:225-35.

Gosnell, Harold. 1937. *Machine Politics: Chicago Model*. Chicago: University of Chicago Press.

Jewell, Malcolm E. 1984. *Parties and Primaries*. New York: Praeger.

Mayhew, David R. 1986. *Placing Parties in American Politics*. Princeton: Princeton University Press.

Michels, Robert. 1949. [1915]. *Political Parties*. Glencoe, IL: Free Press.

Miller, Warren E. 1988. *Without Consent*. 1988. Lexington: University of Kentucky Press.

Miller, Warren E., and Jennings, M. Kent. 1986. *Parties in Transition*. New York: Russell Sage Foundation.

Ostrogorski, M. 1964. [1902]. *Democracy and the Organization of Political Parties*. Garden City, NY: Doubleday.

Pomper, Gerald M., ed. 1980. *Party Renewal in America*. New York: Praeger.

Schwartz, Mildred A. 1990. *The Party Network*. Madison: University of Wisconsin Press.

Wilson, James Q. 1962. *The Amateur Democrat*. Chicago: University of Chicago Press.

2

Political Parties and Congressional Elections: Out of the Eighties and Into the Nineties

Paul S. Herrnson

The 1980s were banner years for party organizations in the United States. They followed a twenty-year period in which the parties were routinely described as moribund and lacking the organizational strength to play a significant role in elections. During the late 1970s and early 1980s the parties began to exhibit new life, increasing their treasuries, organizational capacities, and campaign-related activities. In the mid-1980s, the parties continued to develop, improving their campaign strategies and learning to target their resources more effectively. As the 1990s approached, however, party activity began to decline from the heights exhibited in the middle of the decade, leaving political observers to speculate whether the parties' revitalization was little more than a short-term phenomenon that would fade away along with the intense political competition associated with the Reagan era. This essay explores some of the developments associated with the strengthening of American party organizations in the 1980s, speculates about how we can expect the parties to fare in the 1990s, and suggests some new directions for research. It focuses on party organizations at the national level--the Democratic and Republican national, congressional, and senatorial campaign committees--and their roles in congressional elections.

Recent Trends

The Democratic and Republican national, congressional, and senatorial campaign committees exhibited new vitality during the late 1970s and early 1980s. They improved their fundraising, increased their institutional resources, and expanded their roles in congressional elections. Later in the decade, the parties suffered some financial setbacks as a result of a general slump in direct-mail fundraising. Yet they remained major players in congressional elections.

Fundraising. Party fundraising improved greatly during the late 1970s and early 1980s. Several patterns are evident in the data presented in Table 2.1. The Republicans consistently raised far more money than the Democrats. Democratic and Republican national committee (DNC and RNC) receipts followed a four-year cycle, rising in presidential election years and falling during midterm years. Republican revenues peaked at $245.9 million in 1984 and then declined.[1] Democratic revenues peaked four years later at $81.1 million, and then fell by nearly half.

The trends in party finances are closely tied to developments in direct-mail fundraising. The Federal Election Campaign Act and its amendments (FECA), and improvements in computer technology, provided the parties with both the incentives and the means to raise small sums of money from large groups of people. The new law placed a ceiling of $20,000 per year on individual contributions to the national parties and effectively barred unions, corporations, and other groups from contributing treasury money to the parties' federal campaign accounts, thereby depriving the parties of some traditional sources of revenue.[2] Advances in data processing, high-speed printing, and reduced postage rates made direct-mail fundraising highly feasible and more attractive. This confluence of forces encouraged the parties to aggressively pursue small contributions from middle-class supporters. By 1980 the RNC, which had experimented with a large-scale direct-mail fundraising program in the 1960s, succeeded in raising roughly 70 percent of its budget in the form of contributions averaging about $29 (Adamany 1984).

Table 2.1 National Party Organization Receipts, 1976-1990 (in millions)

Party	1976	1978	1980	1982	1984	1986	1988	1990
Democratic								
DNC	$ 13.1	$ 11.3	$ 15.4	$ 16.5	$ 46.6	$ 17.2	$ 52.3	$ 14.5
DCCC	.9	2.8	2.9	6.5	10.4	12.3	12.5	9.1
DSCC	1.0	.3	1.7	5.6	8.9	13.4	16.3	17.5
Total	$ 15.0	$ 14.4	$ 20.0	$ 28.6	$ 65.9	$ 42.9	$ 81.1	$ 41.1
Republican								
RNC	$ 29.1	$ 34.2	$ 77.8	$ 84.1	$105.9	$ 83.8	$ 91.0	$ 68.7
NRCC	12.2	14.1	20.3	58.0	58.3	39.8	34.5	33.8
NRSC	1.8	10.9	6.0	48.9	81.7	86.1	65.9	65.1
Total	$ 43.1	$ 59.2	$120.4	$191.0	$245.9	$209.7	$191.4	$167.6

Source: Federal Election Commission.

Other Republican national organizations also raised large sums from direct mail. The Democratic committees never matched the Republicans' direct-mail fundraising record, but by 1984 they, too, had successfully raised substantial sums in small contributions.

When the direct-mail fundraising industry began to founder in the late 1980s, the parties experimented with telephone solicitations, geodemographic targeting, and other innovations to try to reverse the decline in small contributions. They also turned increasingly to wealthy contributors for support, and began to rely more on fundraising dinners, cocktail parties, and other traditional approaches. Nevertheless, large contributions have not completely offset the decline in small contributions.

Infrastructure and Staff. Good fiscal health provided the foundation for major organizational development during the late 1970s and early-to-mid-1980s. Specialization, professionalism, and organizational expansion became the orders of the day at the parties' national, congressional, and senatorial campaign committees (Cotter and Bibby 1980; Conway 1983; Kayden and Mahe 1985; Herrnson 1988; Sabato 1988; Frantzich 1989). The decade began with only two organizations, the RNC and the National Republican Congressional Committee (NRCC), housed in party-owned buildings. Following the 1984 election, the three Democratic national party organizations moved into the new Democratic Headquarters Building. The National Republican Senatorial Committee (NRSC) moved into the plush Ronald Reagan Center in December of 1988. The headquarters buildings provide the committees with convenient and secure locations for holding fundraising events, conducting meetings, and housing computer, radio, television, and other campaign equipment. For many political practitioners and observers, the buildings have come to symbolize the emergence of national party organizations as important players in electoral politics.

National party staffing followed trends similar to those for party fundraising, both in terms of growth and professionalism. The RNC, NRCC, and NRSC had a total of 40 full-time employees in 1972, enjoyed continuous staff growth through 1984, and then experienced a mixed pattern of cut backs and growth (see Table 2.2). The Democratic committees, which like to bill themselves as "lean, mean political machines," employed a total of 39 full-time staff in 1972 and peaked at 290 employees in 1988, after which the DNC and DSCC enacted modest staff cuts. With the exception of some administrative staff, most employees were, and continue to be, skilled political professionals who performed fundraising, research, communications, and campaign activities. The staffs played critical roles in strategic planning, advising candidates, distributing campaign money and services, as well as fundraising and running the committees' day-to-day operations throughout the 1980s.

Campaign Assistance. Party support for congressional candidates reached unprecedented levels in the 1980s. Party contributions to House candidates,

Table 2.2 National Party Staffs, 1972-1990

Party Committee	1972	1976	1980	1984	1988	1990
Democratic						
DNC	30	30	40	130	160	130
DCCC	5	6	26	45	80	80
DSCC	4	5	20	32	50	45
Total	39	41	86	207	290	255
Republican						
RNC	30	200	350	600	425	400
NRCC	6	8	40	130	80	110
NRSC	4	6	30	90	88	101
Total	40	214	420	820	593	611

Source: Estimates provided by committee staffs.

whom the American Political Science Association's Committee on Political Parties (1950) once likened to the "orphans of the political system," were generally above $3.5 millions dollars per election cycle, peaking at $6.1 million in 1982 (see Table 2.3).   Party contributions to Senate candidates were consistently above $1.1 million, peaking at $1.4 million in 1986. Most of the party contributions were made by the congressional and senatorial campaign committees. Candidates in competitive contests typically received close to the maximum allowable general election contribution ($15,000 for House candidates and $22,500 for Senate candidates);[3] less competitive candidates were given smaller amounts.[4]

Coordinated expenditures, which consist of campaign services the parties give to candidates' campaigns, were originally limited to $20,000 per House candidate in 1974 and are adjusted for inflation.[5] The ceilings grew to $50,280 per candidate in the 1990 election. The limits for coordinated expenditures in Senate elections vary by the size of a state's voting age population and are also adjusted for inflation. In 1990, they ranged from $100,560 in the smallest states to $1,210,542 in Texas. If an election had been held in California, the limit in that state would have been $2,146,956. Coordinated spending in House races peaked at $8.1 million in 1984; it peaked in Senate races at roughly $16.9 million in 1988 (see Table 2.3). From 1984 through 1990, most House candidates involved in close races and virtually every Senate candidate in a reasonably competitive contest benefitted from the maximum allowable coordinated expenditure.[6] The Republicans

Table 2.3 Party Spending in Congressional Elections, 1980-1990 (in thousands)

Party	1980	1982	1984	1986	1988	1990
House						
Democratic						
Contributions	$ 1,085	$ 1,140	$ 1,322	$ 1,008	$ 1,259	$ 941
Coord. Expenditures	315	792	1,820	1,956	2,891	3,267
Total	$ 1,400	$ 1,932	$ 3,142	$ 2,964	$ 4,150	$ 4,208
Republican						
Contributions	$ 3,807	$ 4,989	$ 4,207	$ 2,612	$ 2,657	$ 2,027
Coord. Expenditures	2,357	5,543	6,309	4,194	4,162	$ 3,001
Total	$ 6,164	$10,532	$10,516	$ 7,806	$ 6,819	$ 5,028
Senate						
Democratic						
Contributions	$ 583	$ 546	$ 476	$ 649	$ 502	$ 510
Coord. Expenditures	2,403	1,216	4,405	6,657	6,592	5,193
Total	$ 2,986	$ 1,762	$ 4,881	$ 7,306	$ 7,094	$ 5,703
Republican						
Contributions	$ 637	$ 701	$ 667	$ 786	$ 719	$ 859
Coord. Expenditures	8,742	5,454	6,673	10,128	10,261	7,721
Total	$ 9,379	$ 6,155	$ 7,340	$10,914	$10,980	$ 8,580

Source: Federal Election Commission.

distributed more coordinated expenditures and campaign contributions than the Democrats throughout the 1980s, but this gap has been narrowing.

The FECA limits on campaign spending have thus far made it impossible for some party committees to allocate all of their campaign money to close contests.   The law has encouraged the parties to spend some funds in elections that are not very competitive.   The NRSC, which has raised enormous amounts of money throughout the decade, has repeatedly been in the predicament of having access to more funds than it could legally spend without giving some support to noncompetitive candidates. As a result, it has pioneered the search for loopholes in the campaign finance law.

In the 1988, a loophole was discovered that enabled the parties to spend additional campaign money in close elections using a practice called "crossover spending." Under this practice, the parties' congressional campaign committees made contributions to Senate candidates, the senatorial campaign committees made contributions to House candidates, and some state party organizations gave money to candidates running outside of their state. The Republicans distributed over $185,000 and the Democrats just under $100,000 in crossover spending to 12 House candidates running in special elections in 1989.[7]

Parties distribute some of their campaign contributions and all of their coordinated expenditures in the form of campaign commercials, polls, or other technical services. During the 1980s, these services were routinely assigned a monetary value that was well below their true market cost, enabling the parties to increase the amount of assistance they delivered to candidates in tight contests (Herrnson 1988). Other forms of party assistance were not subject to the FECA's limits, including providing candidates with strategic advice or assistance with hiring political consultants.

Party organizations also played a critical role in helping candidates raise money from political action committees (PACs) and individual contributors. Throughout the last decade, the congressional and senatorial campaign committees hosted receptions to introduce their most viable challengers and open-seat contestants to PAC managers and other potential big contributors. They also routinely mailed, telephoned, and faxed information about very close contests to PACs and wealthy individuals. In 1990, the NRSC had access to more money than it could legally spend in competitive races, so it organized a joint fundraising committee and used its major donor list to help 50 GOP Senators and Senate candidates raise $2 million (Alston 1990). Party efforts to channel campaign money to competitive candidates were most helpful to non-incumbents running for the House, most of whom possessed less fundraising skill than incumbents, lacked the clout that comes with incumbency, and began their elections virtually unknown to many PACs and wealthy individuals.

In addition to providing assistance directly to congressional candidates, national party organizations have also delivered indirect support as part of what is commonly referred to as the "coordinated campaign." This generic, party-focused campaign is designed to help the party's entire ticket. It consists of television and radio advertisements, as well as voter registration efforts, get-out-the-vote drives, and other grassroots projects that have not been subject to the FECA's fundraising and spending limits because they do not mention federal candidates by name. Most of the money used in the coordinated campaign has been raised in the form of "soft money" at the national level, and spent by state and local party committees.[8]

Party strategy has changed since the late 1970s. Prior to the strengthening of the national party organizations, most party campaign activity in congressional elections consisted of small contributions to incumbents. During the 1980s, the national parties became increasingly committed to helping challengers and open-seat candidates. District competitiveness, candidate experience, and campaign quality became important criteria for determining the distribution of party money and campaign services to individual candidates (Jacobson 1985-86; Herrnson 1989). Political conditions and events, such as presidential popularity and the state of the economy, also influenced the parties' overall strategies (Jacobson and Kernell 1981).

Over the course of the decade, the parties became more adept at determining which elections were most likely to be competitive. Improved organizational resources and greater experience in distributing campaign assistance encouraged the congressional campaign committees to focus their efforts on fewer races. The number of House elections the committees categorized as "opportunity" or "first tier" races shrank from about 100 in 1984 to 40 in 1990, and the distribution of party assistance became more concentrated (Herrnson 1991). A similar trend was not exhibited by the senatorial campaign committees because of the smaller number of Senate contests in each election cycle, their higher degree of competitiveness, the higher quality of the candidates who run, and the relative financial strength of the senatorial campaign committees.

Predictions for the 1990s

It is always risky to attempt to predict the future, and academics are usually reluctant to do so. Still, the trends exhibited during the last decade, and interviews held with a small group of national party staffers, provide some basis for speculating about the future of the national party organizations and their roles in congressional elections.

Fundraising. It is doubtful that the parties will enjoy levels of financial growth in the 1990s comparable with those experienced during the last decade. The small contributions that were the foundation for the parties' financial windfall have leveled off for a number of reasons. Over-prospecting by the direct-mail industry has caused mail solicitations, including those from the parties, to become regarded by many individuals as "junk mail" and frequently thrown away unopened. The generational replacement of older Americans also has deprived direct-mail fundraising of one of its most responsive constituencies. The supplanting of confrontational, Reagan-era public debate by the "kinder and gentler" rhetoric of George Bush and congressional Democrats has robbed the parties of the kinds of extremist appeals that are most effective in direct-mail fundraising. Moreover, the Republicans' loss of control over the Senate and their failure to alter the balance of power in the House have removed the sense of urgency that surrounded electoral politics during the mid-1980s.

Although party fundraising has declined, it is unlikely that the national parties will return to the relative poverty they endured for much of the Twentieth Century. Small and moderate contributions can be expected to continue to account for substantial sums of money. Wealthy individuals and PACs will probably remain responsive to the appeals of party leaders. Large contributions can be expected to account for a larger portion of party funds in the near future.

In addition, party leaders are beginning to explore some new approaches to fill the national parties' coffers. The congressional and senatorial campaign committees, for example, have recently explored some innovations that place more of the burden for party fundraising on their primary constituents--House members, Senators, and non-incumbent candidates. Following the 1990 election cycle, for example, the Democratic Congressional Campaign Committee (DCCC) set a precedent by retiring roughly one-half of its debt with $600,000 in contributions collected directly from House Democrats.

The DSCC and NRSC are also considering a move to increase the involvement of Senate candidates in campaign committee fundraising by creating special group accounts that would be used to finance party spending in the candidates' campaigns. The arrangement under consideration would give the candidates some of the responsibility for collecting funds for the group account from which they would receive contributions and coordinated expenditures. The group accounts would enable the campaign committees to take advantage of the fact that the parties can legally collect larger sums of money than candidates from individuals and PACs. The accounts also would allow the committees to capitalize on senatorial candidates', and especially incumbent Senators', fundraising prowess. Group fundraising, it is believed, would accomplish these goals without violating the FECA's prohibitions against earmarking contributions for individual candidates. Barring a major political crisis, the enactment of new campaign finance laws, or some other unforeseeable event, it is probably safe to speculate that the national parties will continue to exhibit fundraising patterns similar to those exhibited in the late 1980s. The Republican committees will raise more money than their Democratic counterparts, presidential elections will continue to influence party fundraising, and both small and large contributions will remain important.

Infrastructure and Staff. Virtually every recent national, congressional, or senatorial campaign committee chairperson has sought to leave a personal stamp on the committee he or she has overseen. Each has brought in new staff and tried to make improvements. Political entrepreneurs like William Brock of the RNC, Guy Vander Jagt of the NRCC, Charles Manatt of the DNC, and Tony Coelho of the DCCC played critical roles in turning their committees into major campaign service centers. Their successors have made incremental improvements by adding new contributor clubs, installing electronic bulletin boards, or adding satellite up-link capabilities and other campaign equipment. Still, there are limits to what can be done to modernize what are essentially modern facilities, especially when financial constraints are taken into consideration.

It is unlikely that the 1990s will witness the same levels of organizational growth that took place during the last decade, but it is also doubtful that the parties will experience major retrenchment. Most of the staff cuts that took place in the late 1980s occurred at the two national committees, and some are attributable to the absence of a presidential campaign in 1990. The committees will probably fill these "empty" positions as the 1992 election cycle approaches. Rumblings heard after the 1990 race that the DCCC was going to shut its media center as a cost-cutting measure were quickly dismissed after Rep. Vic Fazio assumed the helm of the committee. It seems safe to predict that in the coming decade, the Republican committees will continue to have larger staffs and superior facilities, the Democrats will continue to distribute more of their funds directly to congressional candidates, and both sets of national party organizations will continue to harness new technology as it becomes available.

Campaign Assistance. Fundraising shortfalls will probably make it difficult for party organizations to match their previous levels of campaign activity during the coming decade. Anti-incumbent sentiments among the electorate, and the extremely low rates of challenger success in the 1980s, could also influence the distribution of party resources. Party committees are less likely to commit increasingly scarce resources to any but the most competitive challengers, especially if political conditions work to heighten the electoral insecurities of incumbents. This situation is unfortunate because non-incumbents, especially House challengers, were probably the biggest beneficiaries of party assistance during the 1980s. House challengers' lack of campaign experience, connections, and the strength of their incumbent opponents typically resulted in PACs and other large contributors ignoring their pleas for support. If party support for challengers and open-seat candidates declines, then some quality House candidates will probably be unable to wage credible campaigns, reinforcing the current pattern of high reelection rates.

Funding difficulties also may result in the parties giving special consideration to candidates who helped them raise money. Candidates who helped the most may make big claims on party resources, especially in Senate elections where the parties can spend extremely large sums.

Parties may make fewer crossover contributions during the 1990s. Some party staff consider these to be "luxury" expenditures because they are given to candidates whose campaigns fall under another party committee's jurisdiction. It is likely that party committees will make crossover contributions solely to candidates in highly competitive elections, and these contributions will probably be given only after the committees have first contributed to all of the close races in their state or legislative chamber.

Resource limitations also may encourage a reduction in coordinated campaigning. As long as the demand for federally allocable dollars remains high, it is likely that the parties will spend most of this "hard" money on federal candidates rather than on party-focused mass media advertising or voter mobilization programs. These activities will probably be financed mainly with soft money. The parties also can be expected to devote large amounts of energy to helping candidates, especially those in marginal districts, raise money from PACs and wealthy individuals.

It is important to note, however, that some party committees are still raising more money than they can legally spend in competitive contests. These committees will probably continue to under-report the market value of the campaign services they distribute to candidates. The senatorial campaign committees, especially the NRSC, can also be expected to continue to use joint fundraising committees and other conduit activities, and to continue to search for new ways to channel extra campaign money to candidates without violating the FECA.

Lastly, despite their fundraising difficulties, party committees will probably remain important sources of assistance for many candidates. Party organizations can be expected to remain congressional candidates' best source of the technical expertise, in-depth research, and political connections needed to wage a viable campaign. PACs and wealthy individuals are not likely to provide many House non-incumbents with these forms of assistance. Many of these contributors are likely to stay with the incumbent-oriented strategies they used throughout the 1980's.

New Directions for Research

Nearly two decades have passed since the Watergate scandal encouraged the Republicans to begin to develop their national party organizations. Over ten years have passed since their 1980 landslide defeat encouraged the Democrats to emulate the GOP's party-building program. Seven election cycles have occurred for which we have computerized information about party fundraising and spending in congressional elections. Yet a number of aspects of party organizational development and campaign activity remain to be explored. Some of these relate to the trends and speculations discussed above.

We still do not know much about how political conditions--such as the state of the economy, presidential popularity, international incidents, and public opinion about government--influence party fundraising, especially direct-mail solicitations and small contributions. Does the president's party derive any fundraising advantages from a strong economy, a popular president, a victory abroad, or a public backlash against Congress?

We also do not know much about how party finances and redistricting influence strategy or campaign activity. Do non- incumbents receive disproportionately less support when party fundraising trails off? To whom do the parties distribute most of their money in an election cycle that follows the redrawing of House districts? Post-redistricting elections are typically characterized by unusually anxious incumbents, large numbers of formidable challengers, and many high quality, open-seat contestants. Do the opportunities and uncertainties posed by redistricting influence the amounts of money that are allocated to different types of candidates? The 1992 election cycle offers scholars an opportunity to address this question. Longitudinal analyses of party receipts and expenditures could lead to a deeper understanding of the influence of environmental forces on party strength and campaign activity.

Further research on the impact of organizational factors--such as the goals of party committee chairs, members, and staff--could also be instructive. One could begin by examining the career aspirations of congressional campaign committee chairs. Members of Congress are known to give campaign contributions to each other in order to build support for leadership races and prestigious committee assignments (Baker 1989; Wilcox 1989). How do these same motivations influence the distribution of campaign committee money to congressional candidates? One could also ask if the parties' increasing reliance on wealthy individuals and PACs will influence the distribution of campaign money to candidates.

Finally, there has been very little systematic research on the impact of party activity on the behavior of PACs and individuals who make large contributions. Do party spending and networking on behalf of candidates really influence the flow of campaign money? Anecdotal evidence suggests they do, but this hypothesis has yet to be systematically tested.

The Democratic and Republican national, congressional, and senatorial campaign committees exhibited new vitality during the late 1970s and early 1980s. They improved their fundraising, increased their institutional resources, and expanded their roles in congressional elections. Later in the decade, the parties suffered some financial setbacks as a result of a general slump in direct-mail fundraising. Yet they remained major players in congressional elections. The national party organizations will probably continue to adapt to the political environment and to play an important role in congressional election campaigns during the 1990s. Their institutional development and campaign activity remain topics worthy of further study.

Notes

1. These figures include only "hard" money, which is allocable in federal elections. They do not include "soft" money, which technically exists outside of the federal election system and cannot be spent directly on federal candidates. Soft money can be used to improve the parties' buildings, computers, and so forth, and can be distributed to state and local party organizations for party-building programs and grassroots campaign activities (see Drew 1983; Sorauf 1988).

2. Previous law also prohibited corporations, unions, and other groups from spending treasury money in federal elections. However, the FECA created the first agency to oversee and enforce the law. The FECA does allow corporations and other groups to contribute treasury money to the building funds and soft money accounts described in note 1.

3. These limits increased in 1988 after the Federal Election Commission permitted parties to make crossover expenditures, which are discussed later in the text.

4. An obvious exception to this is Wisconsin Senator Herbert Kohl, who accepted no party money or expenditures in his 1988 open-seat race for the Senate.

5. The figures for coordinated expenditures include the total allowed for state and national party organizations. The limits for House elections in states that have only one House member are equal to those for Senate elections in the same state.

6. See note 4.

7. Figures calculated from Federal Election Commission (1990).

8. See note 1 for a discussion of soft money.

References

Adamany, David. 1984. "Political Parties in the 1980s." In Michael J. Malbin, ed., *Money and Politics in the United States*. Chatham, N.J.: Chatham House, pp. 70-121.

Alston, Chuck. 1990. "Senate GOP has a Big Problem: How to Spend all that Cash." *Congressional Quarterly Weekly Report* 48:3087-3092.

American Political Science Association Committee on Political Parties. 1950. "Towards a More Responsible Two-Party System." *American Political Science Association* 44:Supplement.

Baker, Ross K. 1989. *The New Fat Cats: Members of Congress as Political Benefactors*. New York: Twentieth Century Fund.

Conway, M. Margaret. 1983. "Republican Political Party Nationalization, Campaign Activities, and their Implications for the Political System." *Publius* 13:1-17.

Cotter, Cornelius P., and John F. Bibby. 1980. "Institutional Development of the Parties and the Thesis of Party Decline." *Political Science Quarterly* 95:1-27.

Drew, Elizabeth. 1983. *Politics and Money: The New Road to Corruption*. New York: Macmillan.

Federal Election Commission. 1990. "FEC Figures Show $10.9 Million Spent for 1989 Special Elections." Press Release. February 2.

Frantzich, Stephen E. 1989. *Political Parties in the Technological Age*. New York: Longman.

Herrnson, Paul S. 1988. *Party Campaigning in the 1980s*. Cambridge, Mass.: Harvard University Press.

Herrnson, Paul S. 1989. "National Party Decision Making, Strategies, and Resource Distribution in Congressional Elections." *Western Political Quarterly* 42:301-323.

Herrnson, Paul S. 1991. "National Party Organizations and the Postreform Congress." In Roger H. Davidson, ed., *The Post-Reform Congress*. New York: St. Martins Press, pp. 48-70.

Jacobson, Gary C. 1985-86. "Party Organization and the Distribution of Campaign Resources." *Political Science Quarterly* 100: 603-625.

Jacobson, Gary C., and Samuel Kernell. 1981. *Strategy and Choice in Congressional Elections*. New Haven: Yale University Press.

Kayden, Xandra and Eddie Mahe, Jr. 1985 *The Party Goes On*. New York: Basic Books.

Sabato, Larry J. 1988. *The Party's Just Begun*. Glenview, Ill.: Scott Foresman/Little, Brown.

Sorauf, Frank. 1988. *Money in American Elections*. Glenview: Scott, Foresman/Little, Brown.

Wilcox, Clyde. 1989. "Member to Member Giving." In Margaret Latus Nugent and John R. Johannes, eds., *Money, Elections, and Democracy*. Boulder: Westview Press, pp.165-186.

3

The Organizational Strength of Political Parties at the County Level: Preliminary Observations from the Southern Grassroots Party Activists Project

Charles D. Hadley and Lewis Bowman

The paucity of scholarship on local political party organizations is evident from the brief textbook examinations that focus primarily on state parties, and include longer examinations of city political "machines" than contemporary local parties (cf. Sorauf and Beck, 1988:91-94; Epstein, 1986:144-153; Eldersveld, 1982:141-148,154-157). The primary scholarship examined in these texts originated in the 1960s with Eldersveld's (1964) thorough study of Wayne County, Michigan, and Wilson's (1962) analysis of the political club movements in New York City, Chicago, and Los Angeles. Though based on a single county or city, Eldersveld (1986:89-119) and Marvick (1986:121-155) extended their analyses through 1980 and beyond.[1]

Other information on local parties comes from studies of local party leaders. For example, Beck (1974:1239-1241) analyzed the interaction of local political party organization and its environment with a national random sample of 123 Democratic and Republican Party county chairs in 1964. In the pre-1965 Voting Rights Act era, he found both political parties in the South better organized in the electorally competitive counties. Cotter, Gibson, Bibby, and Huckshorn (1984:57) went on to survey the 7,300 party county chairs or their equivalents in all 50 states. They concluded that most local parties sustain relatively high levels of programmatic activity; that local party strength varied significantly by state rather than by party; that local party strength was relatively independent of state party strength; and, importantly, that local parties were not less active than they were two decades earlier. Along these lines, Mayhew (1986:196-332) exhaustively reviewed the literature on state and local political parties, developed Traditional Party Organization or party strength scores for each of the 50 states, and analyzed them in relation to several environmental factors.

Still other scholars analyzed surveys with local party activists who attended state conventions. Abramowitz, McGlennon, and Rapoport in Virginia, along with colleagues in other states,[2] surveyed local party activists who attended state conventions held to select delegates to the national party conventions in 1980. The findings of this research concerns participation, incentives/motivations, group support, issues and ideology (Rapoport, Abramowitz, and McGlennon (1986); Abramowitz and Stone (1984)). Baker, Hadley, Steed, and Moreland (1990), along with colleagues in other southern states,[3] surveyed local party activists who attended 1984 state conventions. This research focused on themes common to the study of southern politics, including party reform, partisan coalitions, and cultural change.

Southern Grassroots Party Activists Project

The Southern Grassroots Party Activists Project is a collegial effort,[4] directed by the authors and supported by a grant from the National Science Foundation,[5] to survey members of county political party organizations or their equivalent in the states of the former Confederacy. The survey instrument was developed from the scholarship previously cited and field tested in Florida (cf. Hulbary, Kelley, and Bowman (1989)) and South Carolina a year or more in advance of the NSF grant application.

The immediate research goal is to describe contemporary party activism and organization in a region undergoing significant political transition, and where grassroots change in party organizations is likely to have an impact on national politics. The project offers the possibility for analyzing the linkage role of political parties at the grassroots and on a statewide and regional basis. This research is expected to give insight into the relationship of political parties to other linkage institutions such as campaign organizations and interest groups. Also, the study should encourage replication over time because of its broad data baseline. Hopefully, this study will have a catalytic effect on systematic field research about political parties in other regions of the country.

Preliminary Observations on Party Organizational Strength

Based on *organizational complexity* (accessible party headquarters, division of labor, party budgets, and professional leadership) and *programmatic capacity* (institutional support activity and candidate-directed activity), Cotter, Gibson, Bibby, and Huckshorn (1984:28-30) found "generally that Democratic state party organizations are substantially weaker than their Republican counterparts," a phenomenon that did not vary with region of the county. In fact, the weakest state Democratic parties among the southern states were those of Mississippi, Louisiana, and Tennessee, while those of North Carolina, South Carolina, and Texas were classified "moderately weak," and those of Georgia, Virginia and Florida "moderately strong."[6] Every Republican party in the region, in contrast, was classified "moderately strong."

At the county level, in contrast, Republican parties were stronger than their Democratic counterparts in seven of the eleven southern states, though **both** political parties in six states[7] were among the weakest in the country at that level, regardless of the relationship to each other. (Cotter, Gibson, Bibby, and Huckshorn (1984:52-53)).   In fact, the county Louisiana Democratic parties ranked 50th, matching the rank of the county Georgia Republican parties. Mayhew (1986:196), on the other hand, found Louisiana political parties the strongest, followed by those in Arkansas, Georgia, Tennessee, Texas, and Virginia and Alabama, Florida, Mississippi, North Carolina and South Carolina.

Similar to Beck (1974), Hulbary, Kelley, and Bowman (1989:8-9) found county Republican party organizational strength to coincide with affluent county population growth, although the several Republican party organizations were not as strong as their Democratic counterparts when measured by organization "completeness," namely the extent to which the party had filled the official positions in its local organizations. In the current NSF Project, the county Democratic Party organizations appear organizationally stronger in all the southern states except Georgia and Mississippi by this measure, while the comparable Republican parties show comparable strength only in Florida, Louisiana, South Carolina, and Texas (see Table 3.1).

Having relatively complete lists of county party organization members is one thing, but their availability and datedness are something else again. For example, the list of Louisiana Parish Democratic   Executive   Committee members was   very   nearly   two election cycles (seven years) old and unavailable from the state party in contrast to the list readily computer generated by the Louisiana Republican Party.   Similarly, the list for the Alabama Democratic Party was available from the party, but was one election cycle (four years) out of date. Although a list was in the Florida Democratic Party's computer   data base,   there was difficulty in retrieving it for use. The Mississippi Republican Party not only lacked a list of its county party organization members, it kept its list of county party chairs in a warehouse. The Tennessee Republican Party only had an old outdated list of county party chairs in direct contrast to its well organized Democratic counterpart. Neither state political party in Georgia had lists of their county committee members nor did the Virginia Republican Party of its county and city committee members.

These problems in obtaining list of local party activists made it difficult to reach the study's goal of a sample of 1000 activists per party for each state.

Table 3.1 The Extent of County-level Party Organization in the Southern States, 1991.

	Alabama	Arkansas	Florida	Georgia†	Louisiana	Mississippi
Democrats	Complete	Complete	Complete*	Chairs	Complete#	Chairs
Republicans	Chairs&	Chairs%	Complete	Chairs	Complete	Chairs§

	North Carolina	South Carolina¶	Tennessee	Texas	Virginia
Democrats	Complete	Complete	Complete	Complete	Complete
Republicans	Chairs	Complete	Chairs	Complete	Chairs

Cell definitions:

"Complete," a list of county level party members was available from the state political party; "Chairs," only a list of county chairs was available.

& The Alabama Republican Party has chairs in all 67 counties and lists of county committee members were obtained from 46 county chairs, suggesting that they are not organized in the 21 rural counties where lists were not made available.

% The Arkansas Republican Party has chairs in all 75 counties and lists of county committee members were obtained from the 33 county chairs where the party is known to be fairly well established.

* The Florida Democratic Party had difficulty retrieving its list of county precinct committee members.

† The Georgia Democratic Party had county committee organizations in 140 of 159 counties, of which 58 provided membership lists. The Georgia Republican Party had committees in 102 counties, of which 24 provided membership lists.

The Louisiana Democratic Party had no list of its parish Executive Committee members. The Secretary of State had one that was one four-year election cycle out of date. The Louisiana Republican Party kept a current and computer accessible list.

§ The Mississippi Republican Party had the list of its county committee members stored in a warehouse. County committee member lists for both parties were one two-year election cycle out of date.

¶ The South Carolina Republican and Democratic Parties have chairs in all 46 counties, but lists of county committee members for Republicans only were only available in 36 for Republicans and 39 for Democrats, both of which include the major metropolitan areas.

Table 3.2 describes the samples eventually drawn. The sample sizes confirm the findings of Beck (1974) in that the two largest, fastest growing, and electorally competitive states, Florida and Texas, have the most "complete" county party organizations in terms of membership.

Table 3.2 Number of County Level Party Organization Members Surveyed, 1991.

	Alabama	Arkansas	Florida	Georgia	Louisiana	Mississippi
Democrats	993	1697	830	*1096*	*605*	1166
Republicans	**1052**	*974*	796	*1017*	478	*1204*

	North Carolina	South Carolina	Tennessee	Texas	Virginia
Democrats	982	**929**	878	1219	*1095*
Republicans	611	**954**	*479*	1220	383

Legend: The numbers in *italics* are the universe of complete party county (parish) committee membership. The numbers in **bold** are close to being the universe, especially for **South Carolina** Republicans.

For **Alabama** the Democrats and Republicans are samples of 1 in 2 and 2 in 3; **Florida** respectively 2 in 13 and 2 in 11; **Mississippi**, and **Tennessee** Democrats 1 in 2, **Arkansas** 3 in 4; **South Carolina** respectively 3 in 4 and 9 in 10, and **Texas** 1 in 5 and 1 in 3; **North Carolina** Democrats include all of the county chairs and 1 in 2 precinct chairs. For **Georgia**, the Democrats are a universe from responding county chairs, representing 2 in 5 county committee members. The number of Republicans, on the other hand, is the universe of county committee members reported by the Georgia Republican Party. For **Virginia**, the Democrats, though a universe, actually represent 2 in 3 county committee members due to the age of the list supplied by the state party. On the other hand, the number of **Virginia** Republicans is based on the list of names supplied by cooperative county/city chairs; therefore, making it nearly impossible to determine the total county/city party membership. For **North Carolina** the Republicans include all of the chairs and vice chairs and some of the precinct chairs.

Unsolicited Comments On Party Involvement and Organization

Arkansas.   Diane D. Blair (1991:7-8) found a number of county Democratic and Republican Party members who insisted they had never held a county party position, let alone knew what the county committee was, and requested her assistance in removing their name from the list from which she was working. Others who held county party positions were less than devoted to their party. For example, a Republican respondent noted that "Most Republicans are trying to promote themselves, rather than the party and its policy," while a Democrat volunteered that his town would be more

Democratic "if the one in charge would not flip flop and play golf so much and take care of election business."

Louisiana. According to a St. Landry Parish Democratic Executive Committee member "Most of the committee members who were active during the last election were those running for public office." The member focused extended commentary on the lack of connection (continuity) between the committee and the voters. In fact,

> The individual candidates don't bother with the Parish Committee. They run their own fund raising and campaign. Based on my conversations with committee members and candidates, the rural parish committee is not effectively plugged into the election to get the grassroots vote out. Very few people in the parish can tell you who their committee member is.

Another Parish Democratic Executive Committee member commented on the relationship between parish members and those elected to the Democratic State Central Committee:

> . . . State Committee [members] [d]on't want thinkers involved in platforms or campaigns. They want to keep people quiet and calm, blindly following tradition and leadership.

Mississippi. According to Steve Shaffer, some Democratic County Committee members did not think of themselves as party activists, and only agreed to serve as poll watchers as a favor, or permitted their name to be used in an election year as the committee officially certified the primary election results. Moreover, a few respondents indicated they were elected without their knowledge or consent.

Tennessee. The following sage advice and observations were offered by an appointed member of the Hawkins County Democratic Executive Committee:

> In January, I was asked to be President of Hawkins County Democrat Women which I happily accepted . . . I soon learned that the Democrat Party of Hawkins County was alive and well, but in need of energy so I dropped out of school to get Democrat candidates elected . . .

> During the Democrat Primary, the County Chair called a meeting of the Executive Committee to discuss contributions to countywide candidates all of whom were in very close races. . . . There was not a quorum at the meeting, but we did decide to distribute funds to the countywide candidates. I participated in that decision (much to my chagrin), but I had been doing the things that a county chair should have been doing and was not about to let those candidates lose due to funds sitting in the treasury.

Texas. According to Frank Feigert, many of the Texas respondents commented that they were motivated by single issues rather than political party, including a Republican County Chair who "voted for the man and not the party." Such motivation is noted below:

> Prior to my involvement, my daughter held the office I now hold. *We wanted to keep it in the family.* Twice I have been on the ballot and won.

> While I'm sure some people use politics to better their business or own political ambition, I do what I do because I'm *concerned about the low moral goals* of this country and because I enjoy doing something besides writing letters that get nothing more than a form letter acknowledgement. [A]nd while you cannot legislate morality, I am *tired of my tax money being used to pay for "gay art" "free abortions" and so forth.* I think you get my drift.

Having grown up in a politically active Democratic family, including a mother who was elected County Treasurer, the Hartley County Republican Chair explained:

> When I began to believe that the Democratic Party was not responsive to the interests of this part of the world, I began voting in the Republican Primary and working for the party in various ways. To quote from an old gentleman of this community, "I did not leave the Democratic Party, it left me." This is the view of many people in this part of Texas. They continue to think of themselves as Democrats, but rarely vote that way.

She went on to explain how she came to chair the county party along with her duties:

> On my position as County Chairman, I am amused and amazed that people actually compete for the job. I took it by appointment because no one else would. My job is mostly "clerk," finding election workers, keeping records, posting proper notices, etc. It is one of public relations in that I feel that I should promote the party in a positive manner. I believe that it will be harder to find people to do this work in the future because *each time that the election code is changed, the job is expanded.*

Preliminary Conclusions

From the evidence gathered to date, the states with the strongest party organizations at the local or county level are Florida and Texas. The Republican parties in the other states of the South have yet to translate their organizational strength at the state level to the county level. Moreover, participation on a county party committee appears to have an "electoral connection," single issue motivation, and, in some cases, little interest in serving. The county party organization itself may have little linkage to the state or national political party. These questions, among others, will be explored with the data collected by the state research teams.

Notes

1. The local party literature is brought together by Crotty (1986:1-38).
2. The states included were Arizona, Colorado, Iowa Maine, Missouri, North Dakota, Oklahoma, South Carolina, Texas, Utah, and Virginia.
3. The states included are Arkansas, Louisiana, Mississippi, North Carolina, South Carolina, and Texas.
4. Researchers responsible for data collection in the following states alphabetically are: *Alabama*, Patrick R. Cotter; *Arkansas*, Diane D. Blair; *Florida*, Lewis Bowman, William E. Hulbary and Anne E. Kelley; *Georgia*, Brad Lockerbie and John A. Clark; *Louisiana*, Charles D. Hadley; *Mississippi*, David A. Breaux and Stephen D. Shaffer; *North Carolina*, Charles L. Prysby; *South Carolina*, Laurence W. Moreland and Robert P. Steed; *Tennessee*, David M. Brodsky; *Texas*, Frank B. Feigert; and *Virginia*, John J. McGlennon.
5. NSF Grant No. SES-9009846. Any opinions, findings, conclusions or recommendations expressed here are those of the authors and do not necessarily reflect the views of the National Science Foundation.
6. The Alabama Republican Party (moderately strong) and Arkansas Democratic Party (moderately weak) were not matched with their counterparts.
7. Alabama, Arkansas, Georgia Mississippi, Texas, and Louisiana.

References

Abramowitz, Alan I., and Walter J. Stone. 1984. *Nomination Politics: Party Activists and Presidential Choice*. New York: Praeger.

Baker, Tod A., Charles D. Hadley, Robert P. Steed, and Laurence W. Moreland, eds. 1990. *Political Parties in the Southern States: Party Activists in Partisan Coalitions*. New York: Praeger.

Beck, Paul Allen. 1974. "Environment and Party: The Impact of Political and Demographic County Characteristics on Party Behavior." *American Political Science Review* 68:1229-1244.

Blair, Diane D. 1991. "Grassroots Activists in Arkansas: Do the Parties Differ?" Paper presented at the annual meeting of the Southern Political Science Association, Tampa.

Cotter, Cornelius P., James L. Gibson, John F. Bibby, and Robert J. Huckshorn. 1984. *Party Organizations in American Politics*. New York: Praeger.

Crotty, William, ed. 1986. *Political Parties in Local Areas*. Knoxville: The University of Tennessee Press.

Eldersveld, Samuel J. 1964. *Political Parties: A Behavioral Analysis*. Chicago: Rand McNally.
_____. 1982. *Political Parties in American Society*. New York: Basic Books.
_____. 1986. "Party Activists in Detroit and Los Angeles: A Longitudinal View, 1956-1980." In William Crotty, ed., *Political Parties in Local Areas*. Knoxville, TN: University of Tennessee Press, pp. 89-120.

Epstein, Leon D. 1986. *Political Parties in the American Mold*. Madison: The University of Wisconsin Press.

Hulbary, William E., Anne E. Kelley, and Lewis Bowman. 1989. "Grassroots Organizational Strength and Electoral Success in a Transitional Party System." Unpublished paper.

Marvick, Dwaine. 1986. "Stability and Change in the Views of Los Angeles Party Activists, 1968-1980." In William Crotty, ed., *Political Parties in Local Areas*. Knoxville, TN: University of Tennessee Press, pp. 121-156.

Mayhew, David R. 1986. *Placing Parties in American Politics*. Princeton: Princeton University Press.

Rapoport, Ronald B., Alan I. Abramowitz, and John McGlennon. 1986. *The Life of the Parties: Activists in Presidential Politics*. Lexington: University Press of Kentucky.

Sorauf, Frank J., and Paul Allen Beck. 1988. *Party Politics in America*. 6th ed.; Glenview, IL: Scott, Foresman.

Wilson, James Q. 1962. *The Amateur Democrat*. Chicago: The University of Chicago Press.

4

The Importance of Local Party Organization for Democratic Governance

Michael Margolis

There is something almost quaint in these days of big parties, big government, and advertising agency politics about a political institution that conjures up images of Boss Tweed, torchlight parades, and ward heelers.---Frank Sorauf (1960:34)

i

If anything, traditional city and county party organizations have weakened or become obsolete in the thirty odd years since Sorauf made the above observation. At first blush, therefore, there is something almost quaint about the political science profession's continued insistence that these local organizations form the basis of a decentralized--albeit increasingly less so--party structure (Eldersveld 1964:9-10; 98-117; Gitelson et al 1984:76-97; Keefe 1991:43-51; Sorauf and Beck 1988:72 ff and 483). Closer examination, however, suggests that concern with the viability of local parties relates to a broader concern with democratic theory. Indeed, it is hard to imagine democratic governance in the United States in the absence of city or county parties or the local political organizations that serve as their functional equivalents.

The next section of this paper will elaborate upon the statements in the previous paragraph. The third section will examine their implications for conducting research on the roles of local political organizations in effecting democratic governance. The final section will present tentative conclusions and recommendations for research.

ii

The decline of local party organization over the course of the Twentieth Century is well known. Some powerful city and county parties still survive, but civil service reforms and court decisions have eliminated most party patronage; structural reforms, such as city managers, commissions, direct primaries and nonpartisan elections, have weakened organizational control over elected officials; and shifts of population and businesses from central cities to suburbs have undercut the political and economic clout of big city governments. New technologies, such as targeted direct mail and mass communications, have changed most aspects of fundraising and electoral organization from labor intensive to capital intensive activities, and the necessity of maintaining two income families has drained much of the pool of volunteers that local parties once called upon (Ginsberg 1984; Kayden 1989; Callow 1976).

Years of perceived economic growth and prosperity; decreasing numbers in farming, manufacturing, and mining; expansions in professional, managerial, and service sectors; rising levels of general education and diminished proportions of European immigrants in the population have all encouraged Americans to see themselves as members of the middle class. The homogenization and consolidation of news media have helped to reinforce the dominant cultural themes of liberal individualism and to disparage political organizations associated with programs that distribute benefits to the working and lower classes. Over the past thirty years, Americans' loyalty to and identification with the Democratic and Republican Parties has diminished, while popular approval of the parties as organizations has remained generally low. Extraordinary majorities--over 90 percent in Wisconsin--endorse the notion that voters should select the best candidate, regardless of his or her party (Miller and Traugott 1989:79 ff., 171 ff; Keefe 1991:10-15).

If decentralized labor intensive party organizations are outmoded, ineffectual, and generally unpopular, why not simply bid them goodbye--or perhaps even good riddance? We might note that they are gradually being displaced at the local level by personal organizations of public officeholders and that national party organizations and (to a lesser extent) state organizations are gradually taking over their other functions, such as fundraising, candidate training, and preparation of campaign strategies, information, and advertising. Public office holders and candidates no longer need local party workers as intermediaries between themselves and the electorate: using modern media they can contact people directly. By what better means than through direct communication can citizens judge their merits?

In these days when the comings, goings, and doings of presidents, governors, and mayors receive disproportionately large news coverage relative to the work of legislators, we sometimes forget that the political science literature is replete with warnings that unmediated communication between mass electorates and political elites--especially political executives--can form the basis of tyranny. Modern dictators from Hitler through Castro have made great efforts to assure that their messages alone fill the mass media. Intermediate groups that might represent independent sources of political information are forbidden; only those that reinforce the dictators' communications are allowed (Kornhauser 1959; Martin and Chaudhary 1983). In Western democracies, competitive political parties are ordinarily well-suited for the task of offering the citizenry independent political information. Moreover, because their messages seek to mobilize mass followings, political parties can provide some balance against powerful political elites whose messages tend to dominate the mass media and whose values tend to pervade the political culture:

> Political parties, with all their well-known human and structural shortcomings, are the only devices thus far invented by the wit of Western man that, with some effectiveness, generate countervailing collective power on behalf of the many individually powerless against the relatively few who are individually or organizationally powerful. Their disappearance as active intermediaries, if not as preliminary screening devices, would only entail the unchallenged ascendancy of the already powerful, unless new structures of collective power were somehow developed to replace them, and unless conditions in America's social structure and political culture came to be such that they could be effectively used (Burnham 1969:20).

At the turn of the century prominent political scientists supported structural reforms designed to weaken the influence of local political parties, but since at least mid-century the mainstream of the profession has favored strengthening the parties and making them more responsible to the electorate (Holli 1976; American Political Science Association 1950). The central ideas of the "responsible parties" model of governance call for the party organizations to nominate alternative slates of candidates representing distinct political programs, for the parties' candidates to attempt to carry out those programs if elected, and for the voters to hold the parties responsible for the successes or failures of those programs. In the parlance of our discipline, the party organization links the party-in-the-electorate with the party-in-government.

Without responsible parties, theorists suggest, elections frequently become exercises in demagoguery, and, once elected, most legislators have insufficient means of forging the coalitions necessary to carry forward their political programs. An executive-centered politics results: a politics dominated by presidents, governors, and mayors, who command media attention, and are buttressed by public administrators, who ally with well-heeled groups of clientele. (See Bachrach 1967; Ginsberg 1986; Lowi 1979; Parenti 1988; Mills 1956).

While some scholars have argued that a responsible parties model is inappropriate for American politics, and some have even questioned the extent to which such a model functions successfully in parliamentary systems, few, if any, have suggested that democratic governance can be effected through direct interaction between individual voters and state or national political executives. (Epstein 1980; Herring 1965; Cronin 1989; Magleby 1984). Democratic governance is generally thought to begin at the local level. Here citizens can organize themselves to press their demands for programs and services and to elect representatives to carry out those demands. Here too, the scale of government is often not overwhelming nor is the distance remote; moreover, the cost of entering politics is less exorbitant. Potentially, citizens can engage in a rich exchange of ideas about public policy, a process that can even be enhanced by use of the new media technologies (Abramson et al. 1988; Arterton 1987; Dahl 1970; Barber 1984; Margolis 1979). Viable local parties can function to facilitate such exchanges. While some have argued that other local organizations can also fulfill that function, the weakening of local party organizations is a cause for concern. (Crotty 1986; Lawson and Merkl 1988; Truman 1951; Thomas 1986; but see Gibson et al. 1985 and 1989 for evidence of organizational vitality.)

iii

Notwithstanding the independent and central role of political parties in democratic governance modern scholarship suggests that American political parties can fruitfully be described as dependent variables, responsive to social and political forces over which they have little control. Local parties, in particular, have had little direct control over the development of media that facilitate mobilization of voters with capital intensive campaigns, the population movements that have shrunk central cities, the rise of federal and state bureaucracies that administer entitlement and tax benefits, the extension of civil service protection to most municipal employees, the expansion of direct primaries, the diminution of European immigration, the expansion of the white middle class, the structural changes in the American economy, or the persistence of public aversion to the political parties and to government programs aimed at the less fortunate. (Callow 1976; Keefe 1991:1; Sorauf and Beck 1988:496-97).

While national and (to a lesser extent) state party organizations seem to be adapting successfully to modern circumstances, the "boss" ruled city and county organizations have virtually disappeared. That is not to say that local party organizations no longer function. To the contrary, since the late 1970s they seem to have revived somewhat. (Costikyan 1976). But with the possible exception of the second coming of Mayor Daley to Chicago, there has been little evidence of their resurrection as power centers in the party "stratarchy" (Gibson et al. 1985 and 1989).

Moreover, local party organizations appear to have lost political clout. How many citizens seeking help to deal with neighborhood or family problems, or even to secure government services, now turn to their local party committee member or precinct captain? Local party organizations generally have neither the funds nor the followings to sway public officials. Their influence over state and national party organizations is questionable; resources now flow mostly from the top down. Often, local party organizations cannot even control nominations within their own bailiwicks. Nor do they manage to "aggregate" local interests very well, let alone to offer the voters alternative party programs.

Nevertheless, local parties may still have something to offer candidates. By law, they are usually required to provide a captain or committee member for every voting district, and their imprimaturs still resonate with many voters. Like aging madams of once proud bawdyhouses, they sell their fading establishments' services to anyone who pays the price of winning a primary election.[1]   Studies suggest that compared to the old-fashioned political machine, the revived local organizations tend to be dominated by public office-holders and peopled by activists drawn from higher occupational strata than those of most patronage employees. Material motives have evolved from securing patronage jobs to securing "honest graft" in the form of preferments for contractors or licensees; lawyers and insurers find they can also make useful business contacts; and those ambitious for public office can cultivate potential supporters. For others, local party activity still provides an array of solidary satisfactions, and for some it provides a means of working for particular candidates or for general or specific policy outcomes. (Callow 1976; Margolis and Owen 1985; Sorauf and Beck 1988: 83-91, 102-13; Ware 1985).

Of course, the above remarks contain a good deal of conjecture. As Frank Sorauf (1990) points out in a recent issue of *Vox Pop*, we lack sufficient data on the thousands of local party organizations to make statistically confident generalizations. To carry out a research agenda like the one he outlines to fill the gaps in our knowledge, however, would (admittedly) require a monumental collection of interviews, observations, and documents that would dwarf any of our previous or current efforts. To contemplate such a large undertaking raises the question of whether learning so much about local party organizations is worth the price, especially if these organizations are becoming weak and subservient.

This brings us back to consideration of the role that responsible local party organizations are supposed to play in democratic governance. The responsible parties model calls for local parties to engage in certain activities, such as precinct organization, program development, candidate recruitment, campaign management, and communication between the electorate and government officials. One way of evaluating the applicability of the model, therefore, would be to mount studies designed to assess how effectively local party organizations carry out these activities. Such assessments, however, would seem to ignore the possibility that for reasons beyond their immediate control, traditional local party organizations can no longer perform these activities efficiently. That is, such assessments presume that local parties are independent rather than dependent variables.

If we decide to study democratic governance at the local level without presuming that local party organizations are the independent variables, then our perspective changes. Instead of starting with the organization and membership of local parties, we can begin by focusing on the processes that democratic theorists suggest are critical for effecting democratic governance. For example, how do citizens find information about local policy concerns? How do they make their demands or preferences known to local public officials? By what organized means, if any, are citizens able to consider policy alternatives? How are candidates recruited for local public office? How are funds raised for electoral campaigns? How are the campaigns managed? What are the critical factors in determining electoral outcomes?

This perspective provides the advantage of focusing upon questions of democratic governance that extend beyond the locality in which a study takes place. It provides a broad theoretical framework for what might otherwise be characterized as just another isolated case study. At the same time, it should generate information on the performance of parties in the local political environment. Basically, it allows us to investigate who (or which groups) carry out the functions putatively performed by traditional local party organizations. If local parties still perform these functions, our investigation will show it. At the same time the investigation will disclose the extent to which other political organizations, such as neighborhood, ethnic, or civic groups carry them out. Finally, the investigation will show the extent to which wealthy individuals, major employers, bureaucrats, media moguls, political executives, state or national party organizations perform these critical functions.

iv

In contrast to the general electorate, political scientists display an unusual degree of affection for the American political parties. Our textbooks still describe the parties as decentralized organizations with widely dispersed powers. Notwithstanding mounting evidence of the declining prowess of local party organizations, they still characterize local parties as powerful elements in a rather disorderly general party organization that is "stratarchical" rather than hierarchical (Gitelson et al. 1984:76-77; Keefe 1991:43-49; Sorauf and Beck 1988:128-30). This essay has argued that far from being quaintly nostalgic, the special concern shown for local party organizations relates to broader concerns of democratic theory. Without parties or their functional equivalents to organize and empower the masses, wealthy elites who dominate the social and economic order find little to prevent them from also dominating the government.

Nonetheless, political, social, and economic changes throughout the Twentieth Century have buffeted American political parties and gradually made the traditional local party organization outmoded. National and state party organizations appear to have adjusted to the changes more easily than local party organizations, and as consequence, their influence has increased relative to that of local parties. Scholars disagree, however, over the extent to which local party organizations still manage to function responsibly and effectively. Much of the disagreement stems from the fact that we lack sufficient data to generalize with confidence about the thousands of local party organizations in the United States. Yet the cost of collecting sufficient data to resolve the disagreement is daunting, and we have no assurance that knowing more about local parties will be worth the price, particularly if these organizations turn out to be weak and ineffectual.

The research strategy suggested, therefore, focuses upon the functions that democratic theorists have ascribed to responsible local party organizations rather than upon the organizations per se. By treating party as just one of many local variables, this strategy encourages examination of alternative models of local democratic governance in which organizations other than local political parties are critical. At the same time, it does not prevent us from recognizing when active and effective local party organizations perform the functions in question or when less democratic elites are in control. Finally, because it proceeds from a broad theoretical framework into which scholars can fit case studies, the strategy might encourage more party scholars to devote their energies to the study of local politics.

Notes

1. How often do party organizations publicly repudiate a candidate before or after a primary? Even the nomination of LaRouchites to the Democratic ticket in Illinois or a recently retired leader of the Klu Klux Klan to the Republican ticket in Louisiana were apparently not enough to stir party officials. It was Stevenson, not party officials, who refused to tolerate a ticket that tied the party to the LaRouchites. While the Republican National Party has officially disowned David Duke, I am unaware of any concerted effort by Louisiana Republican Party officials or organizations to repudiate him.

References

Abramson, Jeffrey; F. Christopher Arterton, and Gary R. Orren. 1988. *The Electronic Commonwealth: The Impact of New Media Technologies on Democratic Politics*.

Arterton, F. Christopher. 1987. *Teledemocracy: Can Technology Protect Democracy?* Newbury Park, CA: Sage Publications.

Bachrach, Peter. 1967. *The Theory of Democratic Elitism*. Boston: Little, Brown.

Barber, Benjamin 1984. *Strong Democracy*. Berkeley, CA: Univ. of California Press.

Burnham, Walter D. 1969. "The End of American Party Politics" *Trans-action*. December:12-24.

Callow, Alexander B., ed. 1976. *The City Boss in America: An Interpretive Reader*. New York: Oxford University Press.

American Political Science Association Committee on Political Parties. 1950. "Toward a More Responsible Two-Party System." *American Political Science Review* 44:Supplement.

Costikyan, Edward N. 1976. "The New Locus of Corruption." In Alexander B. Callow ed. *The City Boss in America: An Interpretive Reader*. New York: Oxford University Press, pp. 162-70.

Cronin, Thomas E. 1989. *Direct Democracy: The Politics of Initiative, Referendum and Recall*. Cambridge, MA: Harvard University Press.

Crotty, William. ed. 1986. *Political Parties in Local Areas*. Knoxville, TN: University of Tennessee Press.

Dahl, Robert A. 1970. *After the Revolution?* New Haven, CT: Yale University Press.

Eldersveld Samuel 1964. *Political Parties: A Behavioral Analysis*. Chicago: Rand McNally.

Epstein, Leon 1980. "What Happened to the British Party Model?" *American Political Science Review* 74:9-22.

Gibson, James, Cornelius P. Cotter, John F. Bibby, and Robert Huckshorn. 1985. "Whither Local Parties? A Cross-sectional and Longitudinal Analysis of the Strength of Party Organization." *American Journal of Political Science* 29:139-60.

Gibson, James, John Freindreis, and Laura Vertz 1989. "Party Dynamics in the 1980s: Changes in County Party Organizational Strength, 1980-84," *American Journal of Political Science* 32: 67-90.

Ginsberg, Benjamin. 1984. "Money and Power: The New Political Economy of American Elections." In Thomas Ferguson and Joel Rogers, eds., *The Political Economy*. Armonk, NY: M. E. Sharpe, pp. 163-79.

Ginsberg, Benjamin. 1986. *The Captive Public: How Mass Opinion Promotes State Power*. New York: Basic Books.

Gitelson, Alan R., M. Margaret Conway, and Frank B. Feigert. 1984. *American Political Parties: Stability and Change*. Boston: Houghton Mifflin Company.

Herring, Pendleton. 1965. *The Politics of Democracy: American Parties in Action*. New York: Norton.

Holli, Melvin. 1976. "Social and Structural Reform." In Alexander B. Callow, ed. *The City Boss in America: An Interpretive Reader*. New York: Oxford University Press, pp. 215-32.

Kayden, Xandra. 1989. "Alive and Well and Living in Washington: The American Political Parties." In Michael Margolis and Gary A. Mauser, eds., *Manipulating Public Opinion: Essays on Public Opinion as a Dependent Variable*. Pacific Grove, CA: Brooks/Cole, pp. 70-94.

Keefe, William J. 1991. *Parties, Politics and Public Policy in America*. 6th ed. Washington, D.C.: CQ Press.

Kornhauser, William. 1959. *The Politics of Mass Society*. Glencoe, IL: The Free Press.

Lawson, Kay, and Peter H. Merkl, eds. 1988. *When Parties Fail: Emerging Alternative Organizations*. Princeton, NJ: Princeton University Press

Lowi, Theodore J. 1979. *The End of Liberalism*. 2nd ed. New York: Norton.

Magleby, David. 1984. *Direct Legislation*. Baltimore, MD: Johns Hopkins University Press.

Margolis, Michael. 1979. *Viable Democracy*. New York: Penguin Books.

Margolis, Michael, and Raymond E. Owen. 1985. "From Organization to Personalism: A Note on Transmogrification of the Local Party Organization" *Polity* 18: 313-28.

Martin, L. John, and Anju Grover Chaudhary, eds. 1983. *Comparative Mass Media Systems*. White Plain, NY: Longman Inc.

Miller, Warren E. and Santa A Traugott. 1989. *American National Election Studies Data Sourcebook*. Cambridge, MA: Harvard University Press.

Mills, C. Wright. 1956. *The Power Elite*. New York: Oxford University Press.

Parenti, Michael. 1988. *Democracy for the Few*. 5th ed. New York: St. Martin's Press.

Sorauf, Frank. 1960. "The Silent Revolution in Patronage." *Public Administration Review* 20:28-34.

Sorauf, Frank. 1990. "Studying Local Parties: The Need for Better Data" *Vox Pop* 9 (2):4, 7.

Sorauf, Frank and Paul Allen Beck. 1988. *Party Politics in America*. 6th ed. Glenview, IL: Scott, Foresman/Little Brown.

Thomas, John Clayton. 1986. *Between Citizen and City: Neighborhood Organization and Urban Politics in Cincinnati*. Lawrence, KS: University of Kansas Press.

Truman, David B. 1951. *The Governmental Process*. New York: A. A. Knopf.

Ware, Alan. 1985. *The Breakdown of Democratic Party Organization, 1940-80*. New York: Oxford University Press.

5

Questions Raised by Recent Attempts at Local Party Reform

Kay Lawson

It is appropriate that my presentation be the last because what I have to say reflects my experiences in practical politics. For although I am here as a member of the "Scholarly Perspectives" panel and am indeed a party scholar, the questions I want to raise are those that have presented themselves to me as an active member of a reform organization.[1]

The Northern California Committee for Party Renewal is a state branch of the National Committee for Party Renewal. It was formed in 1980 with the goal of strengthening political parties in California as participatory and purposeful intermediaries (of the citizens of that state). Although many of its members are party scholars, and draw upon their professional knowledge of parties to aid the Committee, the Committee is designed as an active reform group and does not itself produce works of scholarship. At the same time, however, the scholar-members (and other interested scholars) are welcome to draw upon the work of the Committee for purposes of scholarly inquiry. When we do so, as in present paper, it is clear that the Committee's work raises many interesting questions for the study of local party organizations. The four I will explore here are the following: First, what is "the local party"-- the state organization or the county organization? Second, how and when do goals of these two levels differ? Third, when they do differ, what methods can and does each employ to accomplish its ends? Fourth, what role can multi-partisan academic reform groups play in strengthening grassroots party democracy?

The Northern California Committee for Party Renewal tends to view parties from what I have elsewhere termed a *linkage* prospective: we believe that parties are the only organizations capable of linking citizens to the state by selecting officials accountable to substantive but changeable programs that have been formulated by party members and approved by a majority of the electorate. We distinguish between the organizational and the public functions of parties: we believe that although parties themselves may seek only to win elections and obtain power, it is the responsibility of the public, i.e., of the citizens in a democracy, to insist that their parties also perform the function of linkage. We believe that no other institution can take the place of parties as agencies of linkage: campaigns and elections have been turned into spectator sports by entertainment-minded media; individual elected officials, however well-intentioned, lack the organized support of like-minded men and women necessary to turn promise into policy; single-issue interest groups lack the equally necessary breadth of representativeness; and even the most well-meaning bureaucrats inevitably lose sight of a larger and possibly changing public interest, limited as they are by the language of statutes already on the books.

Finally, we believe that it is obvious that democratic linkage must begin at the base and cannot be imposed from above by national party leaders who believe they know best the interests of those they would have as followers. Such leaders can offer realistic advice and substantive help regarding how to win elections--without which effective linkage is of course impossible--and can help shape grassroots interests into winning programs. But in a democracy every citizen is entitled to access to an arena in which a broad range of interests are articulated and the process of interest aggregation is begun. That means strong local parties.

So much for our rhetoric. What about our acts? Our job, seeking to strengthen local parties as agencies of linkage, is especially difficult in California. The Progressive reforms of 1910-1912 prohibited parties from participating in city and county elections, established directly elected but all but powerless county committees, placed the control of the state parties in the hands of their legislative leaders, and, by establishing the direct primary, took away the parties' right to choose their own candidates. The legislators used their power to keep the parties as weak as possible. By 1980 California's parties were no longer able even to issue endorsements or offer opposition in primary or local elections and were told, by law, where to hold their state conventions, when to hold them, and who might attend. Party organization below the level of the county was limited to "clubs" (Democratic) or "assemblies" (Republican); both were legally unofficial and neither was permitted to elect representatives to higher party bodies. As the committee began its work, California's parties were so weak as to be virtually nonexistent, particularly at the local level.

The Committee realized it was impossible to strengthen California's parties so long as the legislators' debilitating control was so strongly enforced by law. It made no sense to ask those who profited from the status quo to change it, so we did not take our case to Sacramento: we took it to court. We sued the state of California for excessive and unconstitutional regulation of the parties. Our case, which came to be know as *March Fong Eu v. San Francisco County Democrats*, argued that state law violated the First

Amendment in three respects: first, in denying the right to endorse in primary elections; second, in denying parties the right to endorse in nonpartisan elections, and third, in imposing on the parties a number of rules and regulations regarding their conduct of their internal affairs (specifically, the selection requirements for State Central Committee members, the stipulation that State Chairs could serve only two year terms and must be chosen alternately in the northern and southern halves of the state; the determination of the time and place of party meetings, and the limits set for party dues).

Because the Committee itself lacked adequate legal "standing," one of its first tasks was to find appropriate co-litigants, i.e., party members and units directly affected by the offending laws. It was at this point that the distinction between different levels of "local" parties became clear to us: controlled as they were by legislators (whose exercise of power would be limited by stronger parties holding them accountable), the State Central Committees of the major parties refused to join the suit. (Years later, when victory was clearly close at hand, the Democratic State Central Committee did join the action). Local Democratic County Committees, however, signed on with amazing alacrity: within a month the San Francisco, Alameda, Santa Clara and Los Angeles County Committees were all co-litigants. The Republicans proved much more cohesive on the matter: it was very difficult to find a Republican County Committee willing to challenge its state leadership, and it was only after several weeks of internal contention that the San Francisco Republicans broke ranks with the state party and joined the suit. The Libertarian Party was the most cohesive: from the beginning, its statewide organization was one of the strongest and earliest supporters of the suit, with full backing from its local units.

The suit was filed in the fall of 1983 and victory was won in the United States Supreme Court in the spring of 1988. The reasons for the long delay, and the ups and downs of hearings at one level of the court system after another have been recounted elsewhere.[2] All that need be mentioned here is that owing to various legal technicalities, by the time the case reached the highest court, one of the three counts, the denial of the right of parties to endorse in nonpartisan races, had been dropped.[3] But the Court ruled unanimously that the State of California had failed to show how banning or opposing party endorsements of primary candidates served the interest of a stable political system nor how it could "justify regulating a party's internal affairs without showing that such regulation is necessary to ensure an election that is orderly and fair."[4]

What is interesting for our purposes here is what happened next, and how these developments illustrate the importance of distinguishing clearly between levels of "local" party, recognizing when the goals of these two levels differ, and identifying the methods each level may employ to accomplish its ends.

To begin with, the state Republicans, consistent with their earlier refusal to have anything to do with the case, have refused to employ their new right to endorse in primary elections. This is their right, of course, but they have not stopped there. They have also ruled that their county committees may not issue endorsements, and when the Santa Clara County Republicans defied this ban, the state Republicans response was to ask the California legislature to add a clause to the California Electoral Code stating that the Republican State Central Committee could prohibit or limit the power of county central committees to endorse and that the Superior Court could issue restraining orders or injunctions prohibiting such endorsement. The bill passed, aided by the votes of several Democrats, and although patently contrary to the *Eu* ruling became law without the Governor's signature as of October 1, 1988.[5]

The Democrats, on the other hand, took up the challenge and decided to issue endorsements. However, the procedure they have established is cumbersome (one-fourth of the party's forty page by-laws is now devoted to explaining it), and heavily weighted in favor of maintaining centralized control over the process. In order to be endorsed, incumbents need only a simple majority, but non-incumbents must gain 60 percent of the vote of caucus members present and voting at endorsement caucuses meeting during an "endorsing convention" of the Democratic State Central Committee.[6] All endorsement decisions must be ratified by a majority of the present and voting members of the Democratic State Central Committee except those for statewide office (in which case the endorsing caucus is composed of all members anyway). The Central Committee can decide to endorse a substitute candidate, from among those earlier considered for endorsement by the relevant endorsing caucus, once an earlier endorsement has been "vacated" by nonratification, although such a substitute candidate must receive at least 75 percent of the vote. After the primary, all winners are deemed to be the endorsed candidates of the party (whether or not previously endorsed) unless 75 percent of the members of the Executive Board object.

In addition to creating endorsement rules that favor incumbents and the party leadership, the Democrats also established clear limits on endorsement activities by lower party units. If a County Central Committee wants to give an independent endorsement to a candidate for statewide partisan public office it must ask the Executive Board of the State Central Committee for a "variance," and even if that request is granted, the locally-endorsed candidate must still go through the regular state endorsement process. Endorsements for candidates for County Central Committees are not allowed. Any unit of the party which gives "an independent, unauthorized" endorsement forfeits its right to representation on the Central Committee "and the privileges and benefits which may be attached thereto for a period of 12 months from the time it renders such an endorsement, or the remainder of the term of the current State Central Committee, whichever is longer."

The party does allow "pre-endorsing conferences" at the regional level. Any candidate gaining 70 percent or more of the votes at such a meeting may have his or her name placed on the "consent calendar" of the Central Committee's endorsing convention, and this calendar is approved by a simple majority vote. However, a name may be removed from the consent calendar by any five members of the Central Committee who reside in the district in question and who file a letter of objection with the State Chair up to ten days prior to the State Endorsing Convention.[7]

As one would expect, the net result of such regulations has been massive re-endorsement of incumbents. In 1988 only one of the Democratic incumbents running for Congress or state legislative office failed to gain endorsements, and that candidate nevertheless won the primary and the general election. In the 1990 gubernatorial race, when the party had no incumbent in office, the candidate it endorsed (by a margin of two votes) lost in the primary vote nevertheless, and the winner, former San Francisco Mayor Dianne Feinstein, went on to lose the general election.

These responses by the major parties also say something about the ability of multi-partisan academic reform groups to strengthen grassroots party democracy. So far, the hoped for democratization of the parties has been only slightly advanced by the endorsement provisions of the *Eu* decision. The major parties have either refused to endorse altogether, or kept the process securely under centralized control, and neither endorsing nor denying endorsement has yet been shown to have a significant effect on the outcome of elections. Yet the process does appear to be underway: maverick Republican County Committees are continuing to fight for endorsement rights; and Democratic Endorsement Conventions are well attended and publicized. Grassroots party activists do have a new arena for seeking greater power within their parties, and some of them are using it.

Similar answers to our four questions can be found in the parties' response to winning the right to set their own rules and regulations. Here too the State Central Committees have seen to it that only minor changes have been made (e.g., the Democrats immediately changed the term of the State Party Chair from two to four years and eliminated the proviso that the chairmanship must alternate between northern and southern California). And the parties' legislators have written new legislation regulating the parties in a detailed (not to say nit-picking) fashion which appears to be clearly contrary to the *Eu* decision.[8]

The legislators (who continue to control the parties' State Central Committees) have also used extravagantly dilatory tactics to delay the removal of even those clauses in the California Elections Code that were specifically named as unconstitutional by the *Eu* decision. Even after the victors in the lawsuit "entered into stipulation," a legal process seeking an order to enforce a judicial decision, and won an order invalidating (again!) all such sections of the Code, the provisions remained in the Code, and continued to be enforced by county clerks and elections officials who were apparently unaware of either the decision or the stipulation. In 1990, a bill was introduced to eliminate all sections of the Code relating to the Republican and Democratic Parties that had been specifically invalidated by the *Eu* decision, plus additional sections that made no sense without those already invalidated. The Republicans in the legislature, embroiled in their internal battles over the matter of endorsement, decided to take no part in this legislation. The bill passed nevertheless in the Assembly, but when it reached the State Senate questions were raised about the need to eliminate similar laws regulating the Peace and Freedom, Libertarian, and American Independent Party as well. Rather than address that matter, the Senate gutted the bill by amendment: in its final version the law simply required the State Central Committee of the Democratic Party to convene in Sacramento after a general election in March rather than between January and March![9]

If victory at the level of the U. S. Supreme Court is so slow in producing effective change, are other means open to would-be reformers? The Committee put the matter to the test in spring 1991, seeking to rally support for a change in California's method of delegate selection. Backed by former Governor Jerry Brown (for reasons undoubtedly his own), the Committee recommended to the Democratic Party (assuming the Republican Party would be forced to follow suit) that it select its convention delegates by a mixed system, half primary and half caucus. Telephone interviews with party leaders in caucus states convinced Committee members that when properly organized, the caucus system is more democratic than media-manipulated primaries and is an effective way of building strong local parties. The idea also appealed to many in the party who had no particular interest in these goals, simply because caucus delegates could be chosen in March. California law, seemingly unchangeable at least for the immediate future, mandates that the primary be held in June, which means that the nation's largest state usually has no influence whatsoever on the national outcome. Changing to the mixed system would give California the voice it now lacks.

However, although the new idea won considerable grassroots support, particularly in Northern California, and a resolution proposing that a plan for such a system be formulated and given serious consideration passed at the Democratic Party's 1991 statewide convention, all the cards proved to be on the other side. It soon became clear that most of the state party leaders (including Jerry Brown's successor as chair, Phil Angelides) had no interest in a system which might change present power arrangements within the party. The Ad Hoc Delegates Selection Committee appointed by Angelides to carry out the convention resolution was clearly stacked against the move, and local party leaders who came to testify at its hearing did not rush to the rescue; most of them, especially in Southern California, said unashamedly that whatever its advantages it simply sounded like too much work for them. The Committee's two to one recommendation against shifting to a mixed system was adopted by voice vote at the June 1991 meeting of the party's Executive Board.

The Committee's work seeking to strengthen local parties in California has not given definitive answers to the questions raised in this paper. Our work does, however, make clear that state and county levels of our parties may differ significantly and should not be considered indiscriminately as the "local" party. Furthermore, it suggests an interesting range of tactics that strongly centralized state party organizations can employ when grassroots activists, aided and abetted by multi-partisan reform groups, threaten to challenge their control. And it hints at the likely effectiveness of the various tactics the latter may seek to employ. Although such has never been more than a secondary objective of the Committee, its work is raising new questions for the scholarly study of parties, whatever it may eventually accomplish regarding its more purposive ends.

Notes

1. Portions of this article are drawn from an earlier study by the author, "Party Renewal: From Courtroom to Community," in *California Policy Choices* Vol. 7 Sacramento: University of Southern California.

2. Roy Christman and Barbara Norrander, "A Reflection on Political Party Deregulation Via the Courts: The Case of California" *The Journal of Law and Politics* 6:723-744, 1990 and Kay Lawson, 1985. "Challenging Regulation of Political Parties: The California Case" *The Journal of Law and Politics* 2:263-285, 1985.

3. The matter was taken up in a later case, *Renne v. Geary*, set aside without prejudice by the U.S. Supreme Court in a 1991 ruling on the grounds of inadequate standing; a new case is presently being organized.

4. *Eu v. S. F. Democrats*, 97-1269, U. S. Sup Ct.,:15-18.

5. Assembly Bill 4187.

6. Those members of the Committee who reside in the geographic area covered by the office in question form the caucuses.

7. Deborah Seiler, editor of *The Seiler Report*, provided information on this legislation.

8. Assembly Bill 4187, mentioned above, also amended Section 8710 of the California Elections Code to require the Republican Central Committee to convene in Sacramento after a general election between the first full weekend in January and the first full weekend in March, such meeting to "begin no later than 10 o'clock a.m. on Saturday" and was followed the next year by Assembly Bill 3207 requiring Republican certain county central committees to meet on a "weekday designated, by the county clerk, in the week after the first Sunday in January following the direct primary election." cf. California Democratic Party. 1990. *State Central Committee By-Laws* September:24-41.

9. Thus amended, the bill, Assembly Bill 4118, passed in the Assembly, was signed by the governor, and became law as of September 21, 1990. At present writing it appears California will at last put its electoral Code in accord with the ruling of the Court. In 1991 a bill (Assembly Bill 177) was introduced to repeal all laws specifying the times and places for convening state Democratic, Republican, and Peace and Freedom central committees as well as those parts of the electoral Code requiring county central committees to meet in county courthouses at a specified date or at the call of the county clerk. Assembly Bill 177 is expected to pass.

PART TWO

Applied Perspectives

6

Comments by Practitioners

Michael Margolis *(Workshop Organizer)*:

The title of the workshop summarizes some of the issues we are discussing this afternoon. In our first session, we had a distinguished panel of political scientists actively researching parties, and in our second session, we have a panel of practitioners with great and varied experience with political parties. Members of the second panel have read the papers by the members of the first panel and can respond to their remarks if they wish. We will hear from John Pitney, Former Research Director, Republican National Committee and Assistant Professor, Claremont McKenna College; Lynn Cutler, Vice Chair, Democratic National Committee; Mark Strand, Administrative Assistant, Congressman Bill Lowery; Les Frances, Executive Director, Democratic Congressional Campaign Committee; and Tom Cole, Executive Director, National Republican Campaign Committee.

John Pitney *(Former Research Director, Republican National Committee and Assistant Professor, Claremont McKenna College)*:

I am here as a "hackademic." I probably could have served on either panel because I have been both a practitioner and a political scientist. Until a few weeks ago I was with the Republican National Committee, serving as Director of Research, and now I am back, teaching government at Claremont McKenna College.

A good place to start is by clearing up a common misconception: that the Republican National Committee has a strong policy orientation. Many people think that the RNC puts out position papers and indoctrinates candidates into party ideology and so forth. In fact, it does surprisingly little in this regard. During my time at RNC, the Research Department devoted most of its attention to providing speakers with political information and to helping the press secretary prepare party officials for media interviews. To the limited extent that we did produce material for outside usage, our work hewed closely to White House statements, with very little "value added." There was more public activity in the mid-1980s, as Paul Herrnson's excellent paper points out. At that time, there was a peak in staffing at the RNC, and it did a lot of candidate training, including the preparation of issue books. But these issue books were very carefully hedged, and there was no real "indoctrination" of candidates. Some policy material used to appear in *First Monday*, a quarterly magazine published by the RNC. But *First Monday* stopped publication last fall, just as RNC's quasi-academic journal, *Commonsense*, perished several years earlier.

So why should political scientists be interested in RNC? The answer is that this organization supplies a good case study of the bureaucratization of politics. Here I use the term *bureaucracy* in the everyday sense of red tape, but also in its analytic sense, as in Anthony Down's definition: a large organization of full-time workers whose output is not directly evaluated by the market. These two meanings are related, of course, and James Q. Wilson's *Bureaucracy* helps explain why this is the case. Although Wilson does not mention the Republican National Committee, his book sheds light on its operations.

First, consider "bureaucracy" in its everyday meaning. I came across the following quotation in a profile of David Carmen, a Washington lobbyist who worked at the RNC several years ago, and it captures the organization fairly well.

> The RNC turned out to be everything that Carmen had feared--a huge depersonalized maze . . . Ideas, David learned, often rose or fell on the names of the people suggesting them. Whose idea was that? He would joke, we'll decide if it is good after we know whose idea it was . . . For all the petty maneuvering, it seemed to young Carmen--brash, confidence, impatient--that nothing ever *happened* at RNC, that ideas floated around for months, and then disappeared into the ether.

His experience is not unusual. Nearly every RNC veteran I have ever known has voiced similar frustrations and although much of the griping is directed at individuals, the problem is not one of personalities. Rather, the difficulty lies in the organization's mission and character. This is where the academic literature can be helpful.

Wilson classifies bureaucracies by the measurability of their *outputs*, their day-to-day work, and their *outcomes*, their impact on the real world. In this sense, the RNC resembles OSHA (I doubt that you have heard this comparison before). Both are examples of what Wilson calls "procedural organizations," whose outputs are tangible, but whose outcomes are mysterious. Consider the specific case of the RNC. The measurable outputs include: the money it spends, the pamphlets it issues, and the advice it gives. But the outcome--helping the Republican Party--is very difficult to measure. What difference does RNC make? The RNC spends a lot of money, but when it spreads that money across 50 states and 3,042 counties, the impact in any locality is necessarily limited. Did a particular pamphlet change anybody's mind? Those of you who study elections know how hard it is to measure the impact of communication on voters. Did assistance to a particular candidate tip the results to that election? RNC advises campaigns, but does not have formal and final responsibility for any campaign, anytime, anywhere.

There is one exception to this rule: you seldom know when you have succeeded, but you always know when you have erred badly. The most famous example is the "Foley memo" from June 1989. Mark Goodin, then the RNC Communications Director, had probably done a terrific job up to that point, but how could one measure the good he achieved? He put out perceptive memos and pointed press releases, but what impact did they have on the electorate? How many votes did they win for the Republican Party? Perhaps a great deal, but no one knows for certain. But what *is* clear is that the "Foley memo" made questionable insinuations about the Speaker of the House and hurt the GOP badly. Mark took responsibility for it and had to resign. Again, RNC's problems stem not from bad people--there are many good people at RNC--but from organizational constraints. In a procedural organization, managers focus on means rather than ends, and become risk averse. Since one cannot measure the *outcomes*, one measures the *outputs*. So people spend a lot of time going over paperwork and generating red tape to the point that it irritates everyone.

Students of public policy have concluded that more outputs in Washington (e.g., more spending) do not necessarily yield greater outcomes in the field. Yet some observers have concluded that because the RNC employs more people and spends more money than the DNC, it is having a greater political impact, that the RNC's edge in spending outputs supposedly generates an edge in electoral outcomes. But consider the concept of *opportunity cost*: every dollar that goes into the Washington party organizations is a dollar that is not available to candidates and party groups at the grassroots--where the GOP needs the most help. Yes, the national party organizations do funnel aid to the grassroots, but as students of fiscal federalism can attest, resources are always lost along the way.

Republicans have started to recognize the problem. Last fall there was a fairly substantial staff cutback at the RNC. Although it will not return to the skeletal levels of the early 1970s, neither will it reach the gargantuan level of the mid-1980s. This is not necessarily a bad thing for the Republican Party. Ed Rollins gave a speech this year in which he said "The way we run our party has been exactly opposite to our philosophy of government. We Republicans praise decentralization and damn bureaucracy, but we have had centralization and bureaucracy in our national party committees." Thus, there is more emphasis these days on moving away from the big national committee model.

Where does this leave political scientists? A useful way to study parties would be to compare them to other kinds of organizations and apply analytic tools developed by students of bureaucracy and public policy. Those of us in the Political Organizations and Parties Section can learn a great deal from those in the sections on Public Policy and Public Administration.

Lynn Cutler *(Vice Chair, Democratic National Committee)*:

First, let me say that I am new to this panel, replacing my colleague, Kathy Vick, who was unable to attend. I have always respected and worked with political scientists, but I cannot imagine what you are doing in Washington DC in August. I know you are the only conference here this entire month because I could get a parking space in the hotel this morning. This fact either reveals your scholarly commitment or that your travel budgets have been so severely cut that you can't come during the academic year.

I served in county government in Iowa for eight years and ran for Congress twice, but basically I have been a party person, political junkie, all of my life, and I have a very deep belief in the importance of state and local party organizations. My current portfolio at the Democratic National Committee is essentially working with state and local elected officials. I am always surprised to read from time to time that local parties are in deep trouble, almost a vanishing breed. My telephone call list belies that image because local party officials are certainly calling me, letting me know what is going on, and how I can help them.

At the DNC we have been organizing state elected officials for the last two years. The numbers in Paul Herrnson's paper really tell the story. If you were to look at the amount of money we expended in 1990 on the coordinated campaign, it's the first time in history we exceeded the Republicans on anything. It's only by a little over $200, but nonetheless, it represents progress. I'm in my third term as Vice Chair of the Party. Nobody has ever done this before; I keep saying I'm going to do it till we get it right. Because of my long tenure, I have a feel for what has evolved at the DNC over the last eleven years. Ordinarily, there is no history because the staff leaves after a change in the chairmanship. I suspect that's not true at the RNC because they've had the White House for so long and essentially have had the same crew running things.

We do not suffer from the bureaucracy problem Jack Pitney described; we have at maximum one hundred ten or twenty employees. And number is only that large because we recently beefed up our research division. We do issue papers and we do them frequently. The Chairman makes statements on relevant issues all of the time and we are happy to share those with the public, calling them "The Party Lines." They come out on a regular basis on issues or events.

I was first elected to my position in February 1981 when Charles Manatt became chairman. It was a little like taking over the Titanic after it had sunk. I remember going over to the Democratic National Committee offices after the 1980 election and thinking "Oh God, what have I done?" There was literally broken furniture on the floor; it looked like the fall of Saigon. Everybody had left the DNC to work on the presidential campaign. So we started at a very low point and it was very difficult. Chuck Manatt had been a major fundraiser for the party and a state party chair in California. He used his strong organizational and fundraising skills to rebuild the party in a very innovative way. For example, in 1982, in the middle of my first term, we did the first coordinated campaign effort in the state of New Mexico, which was called "State Party Works." We went to all of the players, our Senate candidate, the state party, and some of the larger county parties, and said "We feel there's a great deal to be gained by working together, and pooling our polling, staff, and get-out-the-voter efforts." These are things the Republicans knew a long time ago, and most of us knew intellectually, but found very hard to do in practice. Having been a congressional candidate, I can assure you that when they say "Well, the Senator's workers are going to go in and drive out all the vote in that precinct" and I know that's not my vote, it's a little hard to say "Oh sure, go ahead." It's a very delicate weaving together of people working towards similar ends.

The concept "State Party Works" later evolved under Paul Kirk to a larger program where we tried to get many of the states involved, although the 1984 presidential campaign essentially ignored it. The whole concept has continued to build until what we have now is called the "Coordinated Campaign." Our current chairman, Ron Brown, has a very deep commitment to it. You can see this from the dollars we sent to the states that were engaged in coordinated campaigns in 1990. As you all know, the main driving forces were all the gubernatorial races, along with the House and Senate elections. Now, none of this would work if it weren't for an extraordinary and new weaving together of the three national committees. We have all been in one building since late 1984, and back in 1987 we started a regular series of meetings between the key political staff to pool our resources, energies, and talents. I think that our success rate at the state and local level is very much due to these efforts.

Now you can criticize the number of staff involved and say it's a problem. And it is a problem, particularly when we look at the list of things that we would like to be doing and we don't have the staff for. As a result, my office not only does state and local parties, but I'm the official liaison out to the Jewish community, which I'm happy to do, women's community, which is a mixed blessing, and now we've taken on the disabilities community, which is a large and growing force in national politics.

Our party structure is very different from the Republicans Jack Pitney described. Our state and local parties are very autonomous and we have little bureaucracy. We are very decentralized and we have a big turnover in state chairs. One year there was a 75 percent turnover. This makes the job even tougher. We have worked very closely with our state parties to get them up to speed on new technology, the Coordinated Campaign, our regional training program, and our efforts to get county and municipal parties committees involved. My office plays a big role in doing the outreach to the local officials and their campaign workers.

Because of the lateness of the 1992 presidential cycle, we've been able to do wonderful things in advance of the fall campaign. The truth is that without the presidential candidates in the mix, there is a great deal of planning that can go forward. Under Paul Tulley, our political director, we've had meetings with all our potential presidential candidates and everybody signed on to the program. This means that we will start a presidential campaign well in advance of our national convention, a unique experience for Democrats. We know that our colleagues on the other side of the aisle were doing research on the Willy Horton ads months before their national convention in 1988. We have never done polling this early before now, and we are continuing to build on that baseline poll, so that for the first time the strength of the national party is recognized.

Part of this revolves around the personality and ability of the Chairman to pull people together. Ron Brown is really quite extraordinary in that regard. It's helped with our fundraising, which is going very well. There are lots of things the national party could do that the DNC never did before. We can do advance schools in the spring and we can order an airplane--things that historically our presidential campaigns haven't begun to think about until the day after the convention. Chairman Brown has forced that whole discussion up front, and absent the parochial interests of the declared candidates, we've been able to move very far along. Regardless of who becomes our party's nominee, we will be in far better shape than ever before for the fall campaign.

Mark Strand *(Administrative Assistant, Congressman Bill Lowery)*:

I'll be talking from the perspective of Virginia politics. I originally came from the Long Island Republican politics, but lately I've been active in Virginia politics, serving as a member of the Fairfax and Prince William County Republican Committees, an elected member of the Virginia State Central Committee, an administrative assistant with Stan Parris of Virginia until his involuntary retirement, and currently I'm an administrative assistant with Bill Lowery of California. So, I can talk a little bit about the failures and successes of local party politics. I'm not a political scientist. I can blame you guys for everything I learned in college. I'll just talk from a practical point of view.

I think that the organizational strengths of local political parties have become a very significant variable in election outcomes. If you look at close elections, the relative strength or weakness of a local party organization makes a huge difference. I know all the experts talk about how national parties have become stronger, the media have become a stronger influence, direct mail has become important, and so forth. But I maintain that a well-organized local party will compensate for a lack of money and other resources.

In Virginia, the late 1970s and early 1980s saw a great influx of new Republicans at the local level. Republicans who were, quite frankly, former Democrats, and who were strong workers and ideologically motivated. These people greatly increased the strength of the local parties. After a while some of their fervor started to fade. Then a lot of the traditional Republicans started to reassert control of the parties and a period of intra-party warfare ensued. Within the Virginia Republican Party, as in other parts of the country, more moderate factions fought more conservative factions. I wouldn't be surprised if that was true for the Democrats as well, but from the reverse ideological perspective.

This infighting left the Republican Virginia Party decimated. In 1980, the Virginia Republicans controlled one Senate seat, the governorship, and nine-out-of-ten congressional seats, and then picked up the other Senate seat in 1982. But right now, the Virginia GOP has lost three gubernatorial elections in a row, holds only one Senate seat, and only four-out-of-ten congressional seats. I maintain this turnabout had a lot to do with the decline of local party organizations. After all, this is a state where George Bush got 60 percent of the vote in 1988, Ronald Reagan got 62 percent in 1984, and Reagan defeated Carter by 15 percent in 1980. This is a state with a solid Republican tradition and a strong conservative philosophy, but these have not been translated into a practical majority.

What happened to the local party organizations is that they became candidate organizations. For instance, in northern Virginia, there was Congressman Frank Wolf's campaign organization and Congressman Stan Parris' organization. These two gentlemen operated the only real political organization in northern Virginia. Meanwhile the county organizations and the city organizations collapsed and became very ineffective. We created a situation where the candidates did not trust the party to provide even poll workers or people to drop literature. They had to have their own people and to get those people they went directly to party members, bypassing the party leadership. Virginia Republicans had never had a traditional patronage system like Republicans in New York or Democrats in Chicago, so the strong parties of the early 1980s collapsed fairly quickly. These declines resulted in some significant losses at the polls.

So how do you pick up the pieces? Local parties are not without some important resources. Money and the things money buys are not among them. Local political organizations tend to contribute very little money to candidates because they don't usually have much money. They are not connected with PAC communities for the most part. Weak parties mostly milk the people who come to meetings for additional contributions. Stronger parties tend to spread out to other individuals, but it's usually a very individually oriented system of financing. The one thing that local party organizations have is manpower, and when they can provide manpower to a campaign, they have something to bargain with.

Basically the local parties consist of several subsets of activists. First, there are the Young Republicans and College Republicans who provide most of the manpower. They're the ones who make the street campaigns work. They put up the signs, deliver stuff door-to-door, and make the telephone calls. The Virginia Federation of Republican Women provides a lot of help staffing campaigns, organizing events, and carrying out the day-to-day activities of the parties. Finally, you have ideologically driven people who tend to appear at election times, but do not to stick around afterwards. What is needed is a restoration of strong party leadership to use these resources effectively.

In former days, a strong mayor or other local official would get elected and a friend of his would become party leader. They would then work through patronage and the party leader's strength would flow from this relationship. To a certain extent, new party leaders still gather strength from incumbent office holders. But the key is to merge the candidate's organization with other groups so as to produce something more permanent. Then you have an organization that can be used not only when the incumbent is running for reelection, but for the other county and local races as well.

I'll give you several examples of how weak party organizations create problems even for media and mail-driven campaigns. When Stan Parris ran for governor in 1989, there was a very bitter three-way primary. He had good media and spent a lot of money on it, and ended up winning most of the major urban centers in Virginia. He won northern Virginia, Richmond, and Charlottesville, but he had no organization. As a result, he got less than 9 percent of the vote in the rural areas of Virginia, and he came in third in the three-way primary.

In 1990, when Parris ran for reelection to Congress, this lack of organization came back to haunt him in his own backyard. He did poorly in Prince William County, which had given 63 percent of the vote to Bush, 55 percent to GOP gubernatorial candidate Marshall Coleman (who lost to Doug Wilder in 1989), and 65 percent to Parris in the past. The local organization had collapsed and there was no one to drive out the vote. Consequently,

Parris was only able to tie his opponent in the county and lost the election when his opponent ran up a huge plurality in other parts of the district. The bottom line is that in close elections, party organizations that can turn out the vote are going to make the difference.

I think there is a resurgence of the local party organization in Fairfax County, partly due to the frustration of losing, but also because of a strong leader who emphasizes fighting Democrats instead of Republicans. He's been out there organizing and revitalizing the party. For example, they are having conventions for delegate races where four to five hundred people attend. Several years ago, they didn't have four to five hundred people vote in the primary for these offices. I think the trend is definitely up because of strong leadership.

The number one problem in Virginia has been losing. You can make a great case that the more you lose elections, the weaker your party becomes. It becomes a vicious cycle because you can't strengthen the party until you start winning. The Virginia Republican Party has been disintegrating rapidly ever since it lost the gubernatorial election to Chuck Robb in 1981. It has now lost three in a row, and the party has become weaker and weaker and weaker. This is why you have to break the cycle with a strong candidate, but if you are not careful, victory can become a one time phenomenon. If you don't build up a party organization around it, electoral success cannot be sustained. My belief is that the only way you can continue to win in a state like Virginia is by organizing at the bottom, generating the enthusiasm at the local level, and restoring strong local party organizations. Despite the current thinking from many political scientists about media influence and direct mail, I would maintain that the foundation for persistent electoral victories is a strong local party organization.

Les Frances *(Executive Director, Democratic Congressional Campaign Committee)*:

I'm delighted to be here this afternoon. Actually, I so enjoyed John Pitney's comments about the RNC that I was just going to sit back and let him have another 15 minutes. John said he could have served on either panel, but this is not true for me. I am a full fledged, 100 percent political hack, and not much of a scholar or theoretician. My experience over the last 25 years has been as an organizer, a campaign manager, the Executive Director of the Democratic National Committee and now the Democratic Congressional Campaign Committee, as well as about 10 years in the private sector as a political and legislative consultant.

I'm going to take a different tack, not knowing what my counterpart, Tom Cole, is going to do. I'm going to talk about the 1992 cycle and how we at the

DCCC are preparing to engage in political combat over the next 14 or 15 months. Hopefully, through this process you will be able to draw some conclusions about organizational elements and trends in our committee.

Let me state a couple of obvious things. The first is that 1992 is going to be a very crucial election year. It is the first presidential election since 1972 to come at the same time as a redistricted Congress and state legislatures. We have thirty-five U.S. Senate races, including two in California and in many of the other "megastates." In addition, we have the usual 435 House races, the literally thousands of state legislative, and tens of thousands of local races around the country. So it's a big year, to put it mildly.

On the House side, we plan for the prospect of as many as 100 fully competitive House races. The press has reported that as 100 open seats. Nobody is talking about 100 *open* seats, but rather the possibility of something around 100 *competitive* races. How do we get to that number? I'm ashamed to say it in front of this group, but our calculations have included hardly any scientific methodology whatsoever. There are 300 House seats where one of the following three factors are at play: the 1990 victory margin was less than 60 percent, the margin of victory between 1988 and 1990 dropped by 10 percent or more, or due to redistricting there will be a net gain or net loss of at least 50,000 residents. Taking a look at these factors, and what we know about the districts from other research, we sort of massage that figure, and it works down to around 100 competitive races for our planning and budgeting purposes. These are the races where a major effort will be undertaken by both parties and/or the candidates of both parties in 1992.

It's going to be a volatile election year, given the late start of the presidential campaign, the long term political effects of the Persian Gulf War and the changes in the Soviet Union, and the uncertain direction of the economy. As we sit here, it is impossible to predict the impact of these factors on races for the House of Representatives. Despite the uncertainty, we remain confident about our chances of maintaining a Democratic majority in the House.

We have three reasons for this confidence. First, we enter this cycle with 25 more seats than we had in 1981. Second, while President Bush's personal popularity is high, those ratings are tied almost entirely to foreign events, and thus his draw for "down-ticket" races is not expected to be strong. In fact, on day-to-day issues that most Americans care about, such as jobs, long term economic security, health care and education, the President scores poorly and congressional Democrats do well. The third reason is that the political machinery of the Democratic House, that is to say, the leadership structure, their staffs, and the campaign committee, has consistently outdistanced our Republican counterparts on the critical matters of candidate recruitment and campaign services.

By the way, there is a significant difference between the DCCC and the Democratic Senate Campaign Committee. The Senate campaign committee is by and large a funding operation. In contrast, we are much more heavily into advice, counsel, and helping campaigns develop strategies. Some 50 percent of our effort goes into raising money for candidates and 50 percent goes into providing less tangible kinds of service and assistance.

I'd be the first one to point out, however, that in the last cycle under Ed Rollins and in the current cycle with Tom Cole and Spencer Abraham, the NRCC has made tremendous strides towards eliminating our edge. But frankly, I think that we can hold on for at least one more cycle in terms of candidate recruitment and campaign services. The Republicans will outdistance us, as they always have, in terms of raising money, but I think we will be able to continue to outscore them in local campaigns where, as the phrase goes, the rubber hits the road.

Thanks to the very effective work of Tony Coelho during the first part of the last decade, followed by Beryl Anthony in the latter part, the DCCC has increased its organizational capacity tremendously. It also increased its fundraising ability. Politically, the DCCC played a major role in helping increase the Democratic majority in the House, as Paul Herrnson's paper shows. In special elections and in general elections the committee was deeply involved and in almost every cycle we exceeded expectations. For example, despite Bush carrying 40 states in 1988, Democrats picked up three seats in the House. In 1990 Democrats held every one of their open seats and picked up one-third of the Republican open seats. While those successes were considerable, they weren't cheap.

When we began this election cycle we faced a pretty serious financial situation, including a $3.2 million debt that had accumulated over the past decade, Frankly, it was a debt that financed the political successes of the decade. However, we had reached a point where we couldn't finance our operations through debt any longer. So we've concentrated on reducing the debt, cutting costs at the committee, and increasing our fundraising. We have reduced that debt by one-third, paying off about $1.4 million in the last eight months. We've cut our costs by about $350,000 over the same point two years ago. We've reinvested in and reinvigorated our direct mail fundraising program, which had really much dried up for our committee (though not for the DNC or for the DSCC). We have made a major effort to raise more money outside the Beltway through big donor events in various cities.

In addition, our chairman, Vic Fazio, has done something quite novel. He asked members of Democratic Caucus to contribute to the DCCC and to get them to believe that the DCCC is *their* campaign committee. As a result, we have raised in excess of $600,000 from caucus members. This resulted exclusively because of the confidence the House leadership and membership have in Vic Fazio's stewardship of the committee. It has made a major difference not just in our finances, but has sent a tremendous signal to the rest of the Democratic financial community. In fact, we have raised more money in the first six months of this year than any six month period in the history of the DCCC.

We think we have laid the financial and organizational groundwork necessary to move ahead. Soon, we will step up our recruitment of candidates, which by the way, is a little later than usual time because of the uncertainty of redistricting and reapportionment. We will then begin a very intense period of training candidates, both challengers and incumbents. We will also complete the staffing of our political operation, including a field office for the first time in California staffed by a senior political operative. We'll also increase our direct mail even more.   We're going into telemarketing in a serious way for fundraising and high donor road events featuring the Speaker and the Majority Leader in virtually every region of the country. As I said, I think we are now ready for the 1992 cycle and there is every reason to believe we will be active in the 100 or so competitive races we face next year.

Tom Cole *(Executive Director, National Republican Campaign Committee)***:**

Let me break my remarks into three areas. First, I'd like to respond to some of the interesting comments that I just heard. Second, I'd like to give a quick look at how we organize at the National Republican Campaign Committee, and the third, following very much in the outline of Les Francis' comments, say how we look at 1992.

On the first point, I was struck by some of the remarks about local parties because I really think of myself as a local party person. I used to be a state party chairman, a state legislator, and have not been a Washington operative. One of the things I would ask you to do in your research is to look beyond parties and think in terms of partisan organizations. This is because there are very few successful and politically significant local party organizations any place in America.   There are, however, lots of very effective partisan organizations and I think that's where the Democrats hold a tremendous advantage.

Political parties function every other year at election time and at odd points in between. Other organizations, such as the National Education Association and its state and local affiliates function all the time and in a very political way. I doubt if Republicans will ever be able to come up with ongoing organizations with the same cadre of workers, money, technical support, and expertise. Trying to match the AFL-CIO headquarters with the on and off county GOP headquarters down the street is like sending the militia out to battle the regular army. It's just not the same contest because that union headquarters does something else besides play politics with activists. It fulfills other very legitimate functions for its members, so when it's time to play politics, union political operatives benefit from a lot of good will.

These kinds of organizations are very effective and it has been difficult to organize Republican counterparts. For example, when I was a state legislator, I set up a PAC to help Republican candidates because the party could only give so much money. It seemed to me a smart thing to do, but I got a lot of flack from party activists about going outside the GOP organization. I thought I was putting another partisan organization in place that could help Republicans. One of the blinders on political scientists is to think in terms of parties, not partisanship, which is much more important. Party activists often do the same.

Each party has a variety of interest groups affiliated with it to one degree or another. I think the Democrats have been more successful in penetrating and holding these. We do very well with the Right to Life groups and the NRA. But sometimes these organizations are infused with the idea that they have to be "bipartisan." That's something that the NEA never, never, deludes itself about. I don't care what they say publicly. I can watch the flow of their money and that tells me where their heart is. I say this not as a criticism but as a compliment. This is something our own side has not been very smart in grasping.

Now, let me say a few things about our organization at the NRCC and then about 1992. The question I am usually asked is, "What resources do you provide candidates?" I break these resources up into four categories. The first thing is cash and coordinated expenditures. We can give $10,000 to a primary and general election, and up to $53,000 in coordinated expenditures. Like the DCCC, we like to think we do lots of other things that are more important. It's amazing, however, what the candidates want when they come in. It's very seldom our counsel or our technical assistance. It's often "Let's see your wallet" and if you have some, it's amazing how influential you can be. If you don't give any money, it doesn't matter how good your advice is, it's not nearly as important as somebody else's advice who can back it up with a check. Now, funding is a very important function, and one we tend to lose sight of. I think the first mission of the national party organization is to provide its viable candidates with as much financial support as it can. When we do that, then we can go on to talk about other things that we can do for them.

The second thing we do is provide cut rate services, particularly for campaigns that can't afford the best pollster or the best media person. We have an in-house director of survey research. We can turn around and make an in-kind contribution of a survey that meets all the legal requirements, has got the same technical value, but might only cost $5,000 instead of $10,000 or

$12,000. Those are great bargains for candidates if they are smart enough to know how to use them. The same is true for media services.

After cash and assistance, there are lots of other things that we can do for candidates that don't count against the spending limit. We can give them a research package on their potential opponent, particularly if it happens to be an incumbent, that's worth thousands of dollars. We also have training schools. I happen to think they are very worthwhile endeavors for candidates. These things don't count against our spending limit and don't cost the candidate a dime, but would be very expensive if the candidate purchased them directly. The last thing we can do is in the area of non-allocable expenditures. Here our committee can spend money on the electoral environment across the board to our advantage. These efforts can range from national media efforts in cooperation with the RNC and Senatorial Committee to voter programs where we provide generic "Vote Republican" literature. The NRCC has changed a great deal in recent years. If you had to divide it into time frames, the great divide for us was the middle 1970s. Before that we were strictly an incumbent funding organization. With the advent of direct mail and modern fundraising, we obtained the funds to do lots of other things. We were one of the first organizations to get into direct mail fundraising, ahead of the RNC and Senatorial Committee, although we are now the weak sister of the big three. Since 1986, we've been operating on reduced economic circumstances. There's a lot of reasons for that, but basically people get tired of hearing that some day within their lifetime we will take control of the House of Representatives. It gets harder and harder for us to say that with any credibility at all. As Mark Strand said, our political strength depends on winning. Frankly, this election cycle is a very important election cycle for us. We need to re-establish the belief that the NRCC can make a difference, that we can win and pick up seats.

Let me talk just briefly about 1992 because we don't see the terrain very much differently than the DCCC. I do think it's going to be 100 plus competitive races around the country. I do think we will have a lot of open seats. The normal number is 25 to 30 and I think we'll be in the 50 to 60 range for a lot of reasons. We approach this election cycle with a good deal of optimism and hope without being naive.

I do not think the Republican Party has had a good national environment in which to run congressional campaigns since 1984. The next year, 1986 was an off-year with the tide quite naturally moving the other way. We did pretty well however, only losing six House seats, because all our weak sisters got killed in 1982. In 1988, George Bush's numbers were not particularly good for House Republicans. It was a very intense, negative presidential campaign. I'm not one of those that are critical of Lee Atwater and company because they went negative and won. But these tactics did not build up an agenda that worked down the ticket. I think this cycle will be somewhat different in that regard.   Last cycle, 1990, was another off year complicated by the controversial budget agreement.

Looking at 1992, what makes us optimistic?   First is the President's popularity. I agree that you can't rely on coattails, but I would rather have a popular top of the ticket than an unpopular one. Second, for the first time in a long time the generic strength of the two parties is about even, with 35% to 40% of the electorate with each party. Third, this election cycle coincides with the Presidential election that will maximize our turnout. Fourth, there is anti-incumbent mood out there. Only a relatively small percentage of the American public thinks that the Congress is doing a very good job and that attitude hurts the Democrats. And finally, I think we are looking at a good candidate crop on the Republican side. In our candidate recruitment, we are not as close to the top of the universe as the Democrats. We have more seats that we can potentially talk about as being winnable. Right now we have about 430 identified candidates in about 300 districts around the country and we don't even have district lines in a lot of states. We think that's pretty good. It's well ahead of the pace that we've had the last three or four cycles.